THE
HAPPINESS
HANDBOOK
FOR
HIGH ACHIEVERS

STOICS, CIRCLES,
SHEEPDOGS & AUTHENTICITY

FERGUS

For Tiggs

Connolly, Fergus.
The happiness handbook : stoics, circles, sheepdogs & authenticity.
ISBN 978-0-9600509-2-5
Library of Congress Control Number: 2020910384

Printed in the United States of America
Set in Minion Pro and DIN Pro

Contents

Preface

The greatest irony is that this book on happiness actually began from unhappiness. Not only that, but it never even started out as a book, rather it was intended as a series of guidelines for only one person.

As you'll see, I was coaching a person struggling to understand the true and apparent conflicting definitions of 'success' and 'happiness' in high achievers. The challenge was, this person was both resilient and stubborn. That person was me.

Unsure how to proceed, I tackled this challenge exactly as I had coached everyone else through my career—I treated this as an exciting problem to solve and opened a new notebook to refine my understanding.

As you're about to read, this was the beginning of a wonderful journey around the world, back in time, from NFL linebackers to Chicago taxi drivers, ancient Greece slaves to stoic fighter pilots. Every discussion with gold medal olympians, coaches, Navy Seals, CEOs, neuroscientists, and psychologists challenged and further refined my ideas. I soon discovered I was far from the only one struggling to understand the questions I had.

The more I used these principles working with others, sharing questions, ideas and anecdotes the more I saw how it helped people form their own understandings and find their own happiness. The idea for a book only began when discussions almost always ended with "You need to put these ideas into a book for others." I hope you enjoy this book as much as I enjoyed the journey.

Sometimes our most beautiful understandings come from our most transforming moments. As W.B. Yeats said "He, too, has been changed in his turn, Transformed utterly: A terrible beauty is born."

Introduction

Over the course of my 20-year career, I've worked with some of the world's greatest winners—from renowned professional athletes and coaches, to well-known CEOs and some of the most impressive Special Forces operators you'll never hear of. That's the world I have lived in since my first job in Premier League soccer in the UK, then working with the NFL and college teams, Navy Seals, and CEO's of multinational conglomerates.

Even if you haven't crossed paths with these kinds of people, it's likely that you can think of someone who, in your eyes, has reached levels of great success. Maybe it's a friend, family member, or colleague—in fact, some of the most impressive high achievers I have met are mothers and fathers. Not all high achievers are sports stars, CEOs, or soldiers.

Working with people in these elite fields, I've seen a pattern of the usual expected traits: dedication, focus, discipline, and hard work. Some were born with genetic, situational, or environmental advantages; others were fortunate to have strong role models or mentors. Many overcame exceptional challenges to succeed. Despite this success it will surprise you to know, many high achievers are inherently unhappy.

While it may seem to the public that accomplished people have it all figured out, the eye-opening truth is that many have personal lives in chaos. The CEO of a billion-dollar company featured on the cover of *Fortune* last month is struggling with chronic insomnia and complications from high cholesterol. Another had to recently relinquish control of his businesses to avoid federal indictments. The sports star (also a part-time model) struggling coming to terms with her sexuality and the fear of public rejection.

The NFL head coach you watched on the sidelines last Sunday is on his third marriage, relying on various medications to manage mood swings and sleeping problems. His wife turns to alcohol to cope with the marital tension caused by long days apart. That star NBA player may be celebrating his newly-signed, multi-million-dollar contract, but, in reality, he is at risk of bankruptcy after numerous failed investments and child support payments for children he rarely sees.

These issues are not limited to famous people in the spotlight. The seemingly perfect next-door couple present the illusion of a happy marriage, but they live separate lives under one roof, after the husband's affairs on his 'fishing trips'. Your work colleague who appears to have everything in order and under control is actually hiding a gambling addiction from everyone, his wife and children included. The local businessman with multiple franchises has cheated many people out of hard-earned money.

True success is often not what it is presented to us. For many, image is more important than reality.

"For many men, the acquisition of wealth does not end their troubles, it only changes them."

Seneca

Through my career training these men and women and helping them achieve greatness in their professional fields around the world, I slowly identified an elite sub-group of unique high achievers who are truly impressive: those who achieve a mastery of life, both professionally and personally. These people were happy, or more accurately, content.

These people taught me something special, and this is it:

True success and happiness—or rather, holistic success—comes from living a life of professional, personal and purposeful contentment.

How do you avoid the imbalance? This book provides the guidelines for actualizing and achieving holistic success in your own life, through stories of real winners and reflections on the lives of those who have achieved great things in their professional lives, without sacrificing their health, values, or the livelihood of their family and children. It's time for you to find long-term happiness, job satisfaction, and a healthy personal balance in your life.

It's understandable why we face so much more confusion in today's world. We are all exposed to many more 'role models' through social media, the internet, and TV. Years ago, you would go to a movie every so often and see a famous actor on the big screen or read the occasional article about an authority figure in a magazine or newspaper. But today, these people—and the image they portray to the world—are right there on your iPhone or computer, 24 hours a day and seven days a week.

Whether it is a professional athlete, businessperson, politician or reality star, you can pull up a video, story, or photo with the tap of a finger. The information is so accessible, so frequent. It's so current and readily available that he or she seems almost eerily familiar and much more connected to your own life. Between casual posts of meals and tweets about random thoughts or current events, we feel like we know them. We start to believe that the perfect life being portrayed is real life, when in fact, it is actually an illusion.

Image is not Identity

This is a stark difference from years ago, when most of our 'role models' were friends, family, neighbors, and other people in the local community. In other words: they were actually connected to us and very real. We related to people directly. We saw their failures, habits, struggles—and successes—firsthand. Most importantly, we saw them struggle to overcome the frailties of the human condition and understood that these were normal human traits.

In today's world, we are presented a completely different idea of a role model. Because of the shield that technology provides and the absence of true connection, we are not always seeing the truth about those we view as heroes. We are left thinking: *How does he have such a perfect life? How does she accomplish all of these things? I feel as though I can barely achieve one goal.*

When we don't see the faults, limitations, and struggles of our role models, the mask of their ideal lives grows greater. This creates unrealistic expectations and demands on us, and, most importantly, our children.

"It is neither wealth nor splendor; but tranquility and occupation which give you happiness."

Thomas Jefferson

And technology doesn't help—it promotes social media interactions rather than in-person conversations and doesn't provide us the opportunity or inclination to talk through the challenges we face on a daily basis. Instead, we spend our time scrolling through feeds, focused on superficial subjects.

We often appear to confuse information and data with wisdom —the ability to understand, decipher, and interpret facts for use in our daily lives. The biggest irony of it all is that we have more information than ever before at our fingertips, yet we have far less wisdom and understanding of our own limitations, feelings, and emotions.

If you're reading this, you're likely looking for something more than just the traditional definition of success. In the coming pages, I will help you understand how you can achieve true contentment in your own professional and personal life.

It's time to become content, and truly successful.

THE

HAPPINESS
HANDBOOK

FOR

HIGH ACHIEVERS

Part I
LAWS OF LIFE

"What is success?

To laugh often and much; to win the respect of intelligent people and the affection of children; to earn the appreciation of honest critics and endure the betrayal of false friends; to appreciate beauty; to find the best in others; to leave the world a bit better, whether by a healthy child, a garden patch or a redeemed social condition; to know even one life has breathed easier because you have lived; that is to have succeeded."

Ralph Waldo Emerson

A User's Manual for Life

Did you know that the owner's manual for a 2018 Ford Escape is 514 pages long? It lists and explains every detail of the car, from how to manage climate control to installing booster seats properly —all very useful information on how to operate the vehicle properly. This isn't the mechanics manual, it's the user's manual.

Have you ever wondered what a handbook for life would look like? Not a medical book on your physical makeup, but the manual for life. It would be a guide that explains how to navigate the challenges and relationships you encounter—maybe it would even include a detailed road map for your specific journey. While religion, laws, and rules help guide us through life, no where is there a road map for managing life's obstacles, achieving success, and, most critically, finding happiness.

In working with some of the world's most accomplished people, I quickly realized that there wasn't a singular, noteworthy secret to success. In fact, I encountered many people who appeared to be happy, but were actually struggling with various issues—problems that can arise from the failure to understand the world and their role in it. But many other successful people have found happiness and contentment. These secrets are the purpose of this book.

A Slave With A Limp

Nearly 2,000 years ago in what was the ancient Greek city of Hierapolis (now Pamukkale in Turkey)—famed for its natural hot springs—a slave named Epictetus served in the household of his wealthy owner Epaphroditus. While we know Epaphroditus was a Roman nobleman at the time of emperor Nero, in truth, we know very little about this Greek slave. Even the exact circumstances and nature of Epictetus' education are uncertain. What we know about him and his way of thinking we learn from the writings of his student, Arrian.

We do know Epictetus was allowed to pursue what became his passion, the philosophy of Musonius Rufus, a Roman senator and Stoic philosopher. Few could imagine the impact this lowly servant of the first century would have on some of the greatest thinkers and leaders of the future.

For centuries, philosophers have discussed very basic questions: *Who are we? Why am I here?* At times, we, too, are faced with these very profound questions. One might argue that we don't need to worry about these fundamental philosophical questions, but you'll soon realize that these are an integral part of finding happiness in our lives today.

After emperor Nero's death, Epictetus was freed from his owner. He began to teach philosophy in Rome and continued for the next 25 years, until Emperor Domitian famously banished all philosophers. Fleeing to Nicopolis in Greece, Epictetus founded a philosophy school and taught there until his death.

Epictetus believed that all people should cultivate their personal philosophy—this, he said, was the only sure road to finding our happiness. Most have never heard of Epictetus, but perhaps you have heard of Marcus Aurelius, one his most ardent followers. Marcus Aurelius was one of many eminent political figures who studied Epictetus and Aurelius quotes him repeatedly in his own very popular work, *Meditations*, written during his campaigns in central Europe. Still today, *Meditations* is regarded as one of the most influential philosophical books.

All Is Change. All Is the Same

You're probably asking yourself: why would a book describing how to achieve true success in today's world begin with a story about a slave who lived thousands of years ago? The simple answer is that, while the world has changed beyond recognition, our fundamental DNA and who we are has not. Perhaps it's more confusing to decipher how to achieve happiness, since we are exposed to so much information and conflicting suggestions of what true success really is.

Children today are exposed to social media and the internet, which show fictitious role models and images of health, wealth, and perceived success. Today success is measured more by material or superficial qualities, such as fame or attention. But as Marcus Aurelius, Epictetus, and others found out centuries before, happiness is certainly not based on material things. When these material illusions are revealed as fleeting, people struggle to understand how to achieve true happiness.

Epictetus was from a school of philosophy known as the Stoics, a group of philosophers with origins tracing back to Zeno, who lived in Athens from 335-263 B.C. The Stoics ideas were heavily influenced by Socrates, the classical Greek philosopher credited as one of the founders of Western philosophy.

Stoics believed the path to happiness for humans was found in accepting life and its events as they presented themselves. They believed that allowing oneself to be controlled by desires or fears and expectations were the pathways directly to unhappiness. Stoics also believed we all had an inherent duty to treat others fairly and justly to support society. Epictetus, Aurelius, and the Stoics have had a fundamental influence on many of our beliefs today—from laws and faiths, to the instruction of the world's most elite military units.

> "Learn to let go. That is the key to happiness."
>
> Buddha

"Some things are up to us and others are not." This is what is written on the first page of Epictetus' work written by Arrian titled, *Handbook*. As a slave, Epictetus was faced with the continuous threat of torture or execution. But as author Jules Evans writes in his book, *Philosophy for Life and Other Dangerous Situations: Ancient Philosophy for Modern Problems*, Epictetus stayed calm and mentally strong by constantly reminding himself about what was in his control and what was out of his control.

In fact, only for the recent writings and work of people like Ryan Holiday and Jule Evans, we would never have been exposed to the same fundamental truths Epictetus was. We are constantly presented with the illusion that we have complete control.

You Are Not in Control

Here are some of the things Epictetus listed that are not in our control: our body, our property, our reputation, our job, our parents, our friends, our co-workers, our boss, the weather, the economy, the past, the future and the fact we're going to die.

It's true—some of the things on this list we can influence, but we do not control them. We can influence our body to some extent, by eating healthy, exercising, or changing our outward appearance. But, ultimately, our body—including the timing of its eventual demise—is simply out of our control. Confusing influence with control leads only to a life of constant frustration and eventual unhappiness.

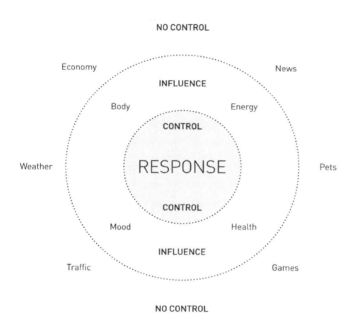

Circles of Control & Influence

In his texts, Epictetus distinguishes the things in our control and the things not in our control. He essentially suggests that, in reality, we have nothing in our power, except how we perceive the things in our life. "We have no power over external things, and the good that ought to be the object of our earnest pursuit, is to be found only within ourselves."

Epictetus continues: "Demand not that events should happen as you wish; but wish them to happen as they do happen, and your life will be serene."

What does this mean? We control how we choose to react to events that we do not control. We do not control what actually happens.

YOU ARE NOT IN CONTROL OF THE WORLD. ACCEPT IT

PlayStation Leadership

The irony is that in life, business, and sport, many of us do not accept this concept of control as reality. Far too often we attempt to control that which we can't, rather than focusing on what we can: the reaction to unplanned events. But most critically (and paradoxically), we become annoyed when things which we never had control over don't go our preferred way.

I've seen this more times than I wish to remember in the sporting world, where many coaches believe they can control a play, player, or game, as if they are pushing the buttons on a PlayStation controller. The best coaches instinctively focus on empowerment and allow the player to do the one thing the player can do—control his or her perception, reaction, and beliefs. In reality, attempting 'PlayStation coaching' is a fool's errand.

The same thing happens in trading and business, too. Many people struggle to accept that while they can influence things to an extent, they ultimately have no actual control over the customer or market. And that's a scary proposition.

The best traders and businesspeople concentrate on themselves and their reactions to events—the areas where they actually have control.

"Security is mostly a superstition. It does not exist in nature... Life is either a daring adventure or nothing."

Helen Keller

While you can make the case for the power of influencing others, it is crucial to remember that we cannot direct the behavior, actions, or feelings of another individual. Across sports—from soccer to swimming, to football and tennis—a competitor cannot control what the opposition is going to do.

I have seen this with elite special forces operators. Novices will react irrationally to events, whereas the more experienced performers control their reactions and emotions under pressure, focusing on the immediate task at hand.

This is what mental toughness really is: the ability to focus and avoid the attempted influence of others. This is why when you are under considerable stress, you are truly only competing against yourself and controlling your reaction to events. You may think there is an opponent, but you are really only playing against the best version of yourself. In the end, the only true competitor you face is YOU.

Nowhere is this more evident than in the final minutes of a game, where the more experienced teams and players refuse to be distracted, even when something goes wrong. Instead of letting a sudden error become the focus, these veteran athletes direct their energy from reacting to the event and, instead, turn their attention to the next situation.

In summary, Epictetus left us with three main lessons:

1st: You must know yourself.

2nd: Understand you have control over almost nothing.

3rd: You have control of how you perceive things to be.

In our personal lives, we often struggle with the most important realization: we don't control anyone—not even our partners or loved ones. The great news is that once we accept this basic fact of life, things become so much easier. As you will discover, this brutal honesty—combined with optimism and a decision to act—are the secrets to success. But it starts with an acceptance of this reality.

Now, of course, accepting this truth is rarely easy, and admitting you have no actual control is often even more concerning. But conceding to this is necessary to not only win, but to also find happiness. As Epictetus reminds us, desiring what we will never have leads to frustration and unhappiness.

Epictetus in Practice

One of the great ironies of life is that for most of us, it takes a very difficult, trying situation (like Epictetus' enslavement) to demonstrate how little control we truly have in life. When life throws a curveball at us, we reach for faith, prayer, and philosophy to try to make sense of the world.

This is exactly what happened to a young American fighter pilot in the U.S. Navy on September 9, 1965. During the Vietnam War, James Stockdale took fire to his A-4 Skyhawk jet and the control system shutdown. He had no choice but to eject. At that moment, Stockdale was forced to face a reality with a skillset he had first learned many years earlier in his studies at Stanford University.

"After ejection I had about 30 seconds to make my last statement in freedom before I landed in the main street of a little village right ahead," wrote Stockdale in his book, *Courage under Fire: Testing Epictetus's Doctrines in a Laboratory of Human Behavior.* "And so help me, I whispered to myself: 'Five years down there, at least. I'm leaving the world of technology and entering the world of Epictetus.'"

Stockdale remained a prisoner in Vietnam for eight years, including four in solitary confinement. He was tortured fifteen times and put in leg irons for two years. He gave credit to his Stanford education of the Stoics with helping him cope with the incredibly harsh realities of his imprisonment as a prisoner of war.

The philosophy of Epictetus is today widely known throughout the U.S. military thanks to Stockdale and his experiences in the Vietnam War. In his book, he recounted his second combat tour in North Vietnam and outlined the lessons he learned as a prisoner of war, including how he used Epictetus and the Stoic philosophy in practice during his capture and how he influenced other prisoners that were with him. Theory is easy—application in the field is where the concepts are proven.

Stockdale's example serves as an important lesson for both people in regular life situations and those in high performing, highly stressful professional roles. As he was ejected from the airplane, Stockdale immediately brought his mind back to the written works of Epictetus he had studied—specifically, the "separate files" a Stoic always kept in his mind for: "(A) those things that are 'up to him' and (B) those things that are 'not up to him.'" In other words: things within his control and things beyond his control. In highly stressful situations, there are simply more things out of our control than within our control, but the single most powerful thing—our reaction—is within our control.

"All in category B are 'external,' beyond my control, ultimately dooming me to fear and anxiety if I covet them," wrote Stockdale. "All in category A are up to me, within my power, within my will, and properly subjects for my total concern and involvement." Stockdale's greatest achievement was his application of Stoic principles in the face of huge hardship, not simply his understanding of the concepts.

"George Bernard Shaw said that most people who fail complain that they are the victims of circumstances. Those who get on in this world, he said, are those who go out and look for the right circumstances. And if they can't find them they make their own."

James Stockdale

NEVER CONFUSE PREPARATION FOR CONTROL

A Natural Stoic

Of course, not everyone has the benefit of attaining a Stanford Master of Arts degree before facing life challenges like James Stockdale did. But that doesn't mean you can't become very successful at managing the struggles of life. Those who are self-aware learn these lessons, often through experiencing incredible hardships at early stages in life. They learn intuitively that the only thing that truly matters is how they respond to life events.

In 1978, the Boston Celtics drafted a young, little-known junior from Indiana State with the sixth pick in the first round. In the 1950s and '60s, the Celtics had already established themselves as a dynasty under coach Red Auerbach, who by '78 had graduated to the role of general manager.

Along with the fact that the unknown junior intended to play one more year of college basketball at Indiana, many people around the league were not convinced that this young player had what it took to be successful, let alone play for a huge organization like the Celtics. Compared to his contemporaries, the kid was good, but he wasn't very fast, and didn't jump particularly high. Combine this with a turbulent family life and tough upbringing, and you can see why there were red flags and concerns about his emotional strength and resilience.

This young kid was Larry Bird—and he didn't recognize any of these concerns. Born in 1956 in French Lick, Indiana—a poor town with a population of less than 2,000 residents—Bird was raised in a poverty-stricken household. His parents divorced when he was in high school and, a year after, his father—a veteran of the Korean War—committed suicide.

Despite these issues that were out of his control, Bird found solace in basketball, and in what he could control: his reaction to these life events going on around him. It would have been easy for him to make excuses and see these circumstances as insurmountable obstacles. But instead of finding excuses, Bird, like

Stockdale, accepted these challenges as uncontrollable. From his upbringing, these events were just part of life as he knew it.

"When I was a kid, I never thought about anything. Never had to think about where I was going to school or what I was going to do. I just lived minute to minute."

Larry Bird

In the summer before he joined the Celtics, Bird badly hurt his right index finger making a diving catch in the outfield during a summer softball game. He hid the injury from the Celtics, fearing it would compromise his value to them. It was so badly damaged that Bird considered shooting with his left hand, if needed. Bird's default attitude was to adapt and control what he could control. The injury wasn't the end of his basketball career; it was simply an uncontrollable situation in his life. Bird focused on what he could control—how he reacted to what he couldn't control.

When people debate the greatest basketball players of all time, Bird's name is invariably mentioned. However, many people fail to remember how the odds were never in his favor from the very beginning. In fact, the world put obstacles in Bird's way many times throughout his life. Everyone seemed to focus on this, except for Larry Bird.

"I wasn't real quick, and I wasn't real strong. Some guys will just take off and it's like, whoa. So I beat them with my mind and my fundamentals."

Larry Bird

Bird is not an exception. Magic Johnson, Bird's greatest rival, didn't have an easy path to athletic stardom either. Both his parents worked long hours. In fact, his father worked two jobs to provide for their seven kids. Born in Lansing, Michigan, he faced racism from a young age during arguably one of the greatest periods of social unrest in U.S. history.

The real secret behind the success of these to incredible rivals is not what we saw on the court, but what we didn't see—how they reacted to the struggles they had no control over before their stardom.

YOU ARE IN CONTROL OF THE ONE MOST IMPORTANT THING: YOUR RESPONSE TO LIFE

Focus on the Response, Not the Result

The greatest learning and most profound lessons often occur during failures and difficulties, not during times of success. One of the common pitfalls in studying prominent people is that we search for the reasons for success, rather than looking at the obstacles or issues one had to overcome to get there. We observe actions so we can replicate them, rather than studying the learning experience from the conquered challenge.

As I started working with successful athletes, operators, and CEOs, I made this mistake myself. I looked for the characteristics that made them successful. After more than 20 years in my career, I was faced with an obstacle and it was only then that I realized that I should have been focusing on what they overcame and how they did it. When I reflect on it now, every single successful person told me this in some way, be it directly or indirectly, but I missed the point every time.

Even in selection for Special Operations groups, it's almost impossible to know who will make it and who won't. This is because the reaction to events during selection is what is important, not the actual performance. Almost every single elite athlete or coach told me a number of reasons why they shouldn't have made it. Rather than discussing this deeper with them, I concentrated on what they did well. I should have explored what they learned from overcoming challenges. This is where we actually learn.

Studying failure and the reaction to it is just as important as studying success. Oftentimes, we miss the fact that the difference between winners and losers is more fundamental—like James Stockdale, it's a difference in how they accept and react to what they control and don't control.

"I can't change the direction of the wind, but I can adjust my sails to always reach my destination."

Jimmy Dean

Shaquem Griffin is a modern-day example of someone who controls what he can. Griffin, the twin brother of Seahawks cornerback Shaquill Griffin, lost his left hand due to a rare prenatal condition. But he refused to allow his condition to prevent him from playing sports. In fact, Griffin competed in track, baseball, and football alongside his brother—all without a left hand. The choice is always yours to make.

Stockdale, Bird, Johnson, and Griffin faced the uncontrollable in their lives, but—rather than becoming consumed or distracted by these situations—they focused on what they could control and how they reacted to these challenges. Some had the benefit of formal teaching, some didn't know there was an alternative, but all chose to focus on one thing: their reaction to what others consider problems or difficulties.

These men exemplify an important point about challenges, because without these struggles, their lives would have been very different. As children develop, it is crucial for us as parents and coaches to allow them to struggle and then overcome the challenges that are put in front of them.

Remember: failure is not fatal. It is actually an opportunity to learn, prosper, and progress. Michael Jordan described it well when he said, "I've missed more than 9,000 shots in my career. I've lost almost 300 games. 26 times, I've been trusted to take the game winning shot and missed. I've failed over and over and over again in my life. And that is why I succeed."

Most reflect on Jordan's great abilities and hours of highlight reels, but what we often failed to remember is that he reveled in the pain and hardship that the failures provided him. He recognized the benefit of the challenge.

The Three Acceptances

While we may still be learning it, Epictetus and the Stoics realized an important fact of life centuries ago: we are only in control of our perception of events and our reaction. It may sound defeatist, but in reality, it's liberating. This mindset is a bridge to living uninhibited —it frees us to find happiness.

1. You Are Not in Control

The only thing we truly control is our belief. While it is only one thing, this is the singularly most powerful thing we can have control of. Our opinions, desires, responses, and choices on how we view the people and events in our life are all in our control. Too many people are unhappy or unsatisfied in their daily life because they continuously and repeatedly try to change or influence circumstances that they have no control over.

The cardinal rule is we have no control over others. Yes, there is an argument that can be made about the ability to influence others—after all, this is why billions are spent on advertising and marketing. However this is influence, not direct control or power.

Relationships and other connections in life give us the clearest picture of how most people struggle with their inability to control others. The most common example is when a significant other has an affair, betrays or leaves, or when a relationship ends, whether it is by choice or by the decision of someone else. No matter the action or behavior, it is important to accept that you were never in control of the other individual in the first place. The relationship is created between two people, but doesn't belong to one, the other or both. Simply put, betrayal is the failure of the other person to maintain their self-discipline.

In more extreme examples, when we are faced with a sudden death or bereavement, it is again important to accept and understand that we have absolutely no control over the outcome. What can we do? We can control how we perceive and process the circumstances: will you live in denial or remember the good times that were had?

If it's the loss of a job that has you dispirited—whether it's because the company closed down or you were fired from a position—you have two choices. You can focus on the event or focus on your reaction to it. In any situation, the longer you spend thinking about an occurrence that was out of your control, the longer it will take you to view the event as a potential positive, enlightening experience that can be capitalized on. The longer you spend trying to understand the other person or directing anger or emotion, the longer it takes to move on with your life.

> "There are more things, Lucilius, that frighten us than injure us, and we suffer more in imagination than in reality."
>
> Seneca

UFC fighter Conor McGregor's coach, John Kavanagh, has a simple but profound phrase: "Win or learn." Whether it's in the octagon, on the field, at work, or anywhere in your everyday life, the choices should never be "win or lose" but rather, "win or learn." Learning means focusing on how you react to it.

You must accept that you aren't going to get everything right, but your perception of a situation can change everything. Having control of our beliefs means we have the ability to process the events in our lives. Will you view the situation simply as a negative or a positive or as a learning experience?

CHOOSE
FRIENDLY

2. The World is Friendly

Albert Einstein once said: "The most important question you can ever ask is if the world is a friendly place." He continued: "If we decide that the universe is neither friendly nor unfriendly and that God is essentially 'playing dice with the universe,' then we are simply victims to the random toss of the dice and our lives have no real purpose or meaning."

This perspective is important because it underlines the primary basis for your mindset: how you chose to react. We know we're not in control, but we can choose to approach every event in a friendly way or unfriendly way. Choosing to be friendly is the second step forward on the road to happiness.

Just ask a man named George Koehler. On a summer day in 1984, the limo driver was waiting outside O'Hare International Airport in Chicago for a client who never arrived. Faced with an uncontrollable, he chose to take an optimistic and positive approach.

Koehler was frustrated and desperately trying to make ends meet for his new business, so he approached a young man who appeared to be lost. Figuring it was better to make some money rather than nothing, Koehler offered to drive the young man to wherever he was going for $25. The young man explained he had just arrived in Chicago to start a new job, but the organization he was joining never sent anyone to pick him up. Koehler drove his tired client to the North Shore Hotel, where his new employers awaited.

The man gave Koehler $50 and told him to keep the change but asked him for his number before he went into the hotel. The young man called him a few days later and over time, Koehler became the man's permanent driver for more than 15 years. All because of one random act based on the presumption that the world is a friendly place, George Koehler became Michael Jordan's dedicated driver.

If you are a pleasant and positive person who interacts well with others, people are more likely to respond to you in the same way. What is reflected in your nature attracts and comes back to you. And the added bonus? The more you are positive towards others, the more rewarding it is to you. And the cycle continues, because the more often we have favorable interactions, the happier we are in life as a whole. You can call it the law of attraction or seeing happiness in others but, in reality, we see in others what we choose to see.

3. You Become Your Environment

If you've been watching all the commercials for genetic testing, you'd be forgiven for thinking your fate is predetermined. Everything is handed down from your parents, right? Not exactly. Although genes from your parents do determine some of your characteristics and traits, how the genes are expressed are affected by your environment. This area of study is known as epigenetics. 'Epi' comes from the Greek word for 'over' or 'on top of.' Epigenetics is an additional instruction that operates 'on top of' your DNA.

Your DNA gets you to the starting line, but how you run the race is up to you. Who you spend most time with, what you eat, your mindset and attitude all influence how well you will run the race more than your starting genes actually will. So now science is proving beyond doubt that our environment—the people, foods and climate we spend most time in—affect us more than we ever realized.

Our behaviors, prejudices, and moods are all influenced by who we spend our time with and what becomes acceptable to us. History is littered with examples of situations where attitudes towards sections of our society became acceptable simply because of the environment and influences of leaders.

I don't subscribe to environmental, genetic, or any simple determinism. Will is the thing. Man makes his character here on earth. I am the master of my fate, the captain of my soul.

James Stockdale

As humans, the people we are surrounded by and the environment we live in can have an unsuspecting but hugely important influence. The people who you spend the most time around can adjust the norm for you. This means that if you are in a toxic environment for an extended period, your values can change based on that setting, even if it's only incrementally.

The most worrying part is that you may not notice how it has affected you gradually over time. Things you wouldn't normally deem acceptable—how you speak to and treat others, for example—can start to feel ordinary or even accepted in certain situations. Like in Germany during the 1930s, the influence of the leader or leadership is an important consideration.

While a negative environment can erode your sense of virtues and values, it is also possible for you to be influenced in a beneficial way by your surroundings. We see both sides in sports, specifically with locker room culture. If a team is very close-knit and supportive of one another, everybody will become part of that group and adopt a similar way of thinking. This is often referred to as the tribe mentality. People will often inherit the traits and demeanor of the tribe, which is usually determined by the group's leader.

You only have to spend a little time around the Los Angeles Rams head coach Sean McVay to see how the environment he creates influences people to do great things. The 33-year-old coach is open and engaging at practice. Players and staff have openly praised McVay for his ability to teach and connect with them. He epitomizes Einstein's philosophy of looking at the world as a friendly place. His demeanor and ability to do his job with good grace engenders a sense of teamwork and togetherness that can carry a group forward in a positive manner. What's the alternative? When troubles arise on a team with a weak culture, where players have varying mentalities, that is when you will see a group unravel and implode.

YOU ARE INFLUENCED BY THOSE YOU CHOOSE TO SPEND THE MAJORITY OF YOUR TIME WITH

Society

"*When, in the course of human events, it becomes necessary for one people to dissolve the political bands which have connected them with another, and to assume, among the powers of the earth, the separate and equal station to which the laws of nature and of nature's God entitle them, a decent respect to the opinions of mankind requires that they should declare the causes which impel them to the separation.*

We hold these truths to be self-evident, that all men are created equal, that they are endowed by their Creator with certain unalienable rights, that among these are life, liberty, and the pursuit of happiness.

That, to secure these rights, governments are instituted among men, deriving their just powers from the consent of the governed.

That, whenever any form of government becomes destructive of these ends, it is the right of the people to alter or to abolish it, and to institute new government, laying its foundation on such principles, and organizing its powers in such form, as to them shall seem most likely to effect their safety and happiness."

And so begins the United States Declaration of Independence. Issued on July 4, 1776, this historic document was born out of a desire to remove a tyrannical monarch and to ensure that a society had the right to life, liberty, and the pursuit of happiness through self-determination.

"What you do not want done to yourself, do not do to others."

Confucius

It is on these principles that most modern societies are based— a desire for a group of people to determine their own future. As far back as ancient Greece, philosophers believed that a society must focus on the pursuit of virtues, rather than the pursuit of material wealth or items, in order to survive, grow and prosper as a united group.

Socrates believed that people should concentrate on relationships in order to develop a sense of community. This was the only true way to ensure the survival of people, your offspring, race, and the community as a whole.

Since its inception as a concept, the idea of 'society' allowed a structure for us to protect the weakest of the group or allow a format for helping people through challenging periods such as youth, or elderly. Of course, not all people share these noble beliefs and it is inevitable that you will cross paths with these individuals during your life.

"Those who study the rise and fall of civilizations learn that no shortcoming has been as surely fatal to republics as a dearth of public virtue, the unwillingness of those who govern to place the value of their society above personal interest."

James Stockdale

Sheep and Wolves

David Grossman is a retired lieutenant colonel in the United States Army who specializes in studying conflict and improving outcomes in lethal encounters. One of his areas of expertise is reducing violence in society; he has written many books on this subject. In *On Combat*, one of Grossman's most famous titles, he describes three broad categories of people: sheep, wolves, and sheepdogs. While Grossman developed this model for conflict, it extends to society and our daily life interactions.

Sheep are loyal, obedient, and functioning members of society, including the youngest and older members. According to Grossman, sheep are kind, decent people with no capacity for violence, except by accident or under extreme provocation. They can at times be weak, easily influenced, manipulated or led. They can also lack the resilience to survive alone or can lose the moral courage to do the right thing under pressure or influence.

Wolves are characterized by selfishness and ruthlessness. They display traits of narcissism, caring only about themselves, often not even their closest relatives. More worryingly, wolves can display sociopathic or psychopathic tendencies. Not surprisingly these traits are common in some political leaders, coaches, serial killers, and dictators.

Encountering wolves, they generally appear in two different forms: in the form of a bully, who will use intimidation to persuade and influence through threat of force; or in a cowardly form— overly affable but deceitful, gaining trust only to undermine and deceive. Wolves, like many narcissistic sociopaths, can be charming, but always with the singular goal of gaining something for their own benefit.

Finally, there are sheepdogs. Thankfully the majority of us are sheepdogs. With a strong moral and ethical compass, they know right from wrong and have a strong value system. They are aware of their duty to contribute to the betterment and survival of society by protecting both sheep and each other from wolves. While determined to progress their own aims, wolves are respectful and fearful of the sheepdog. The sheepdog has a strong sense of not simply courage, but moral courage.

Moral courage is the courage to act for moral reasons, despite the possible risk of consequence. Those with the greatest moral courage avoid the guilt and regret that comes with ignoring wrongs —it is essential for a happy virtuous life. Moral courage is arguably the greatest measure of someone's virtue as is often exercised at the risk of ridicule, rejection, and or retaliation. Of course no one is simply hardwired one or the other, we all have elements of each. Maintaining the character we most aspire to requires constant reflection and maintenance to avoid our impulses.

In reality we all inherently possess the attributes of sheep, sheepdogs, and wolves to varying degrees. We have however the ability to develop and nourish one.

"This may sound strange, but to me a hero is a man who will not accept the status quo if it does not meet his standards... He will stand up and turn his world around."

James Stockdale

YOUR SURVIVAL AND SUCCESS DEPENDS ON YOUR QUALITY OF ADAPTATION

Challenges of Sheepdogs

The most admirable qualities of those with the qualities of sheepdogs are their empathy, moral courage, and desire to care for one another and contribute to the group and society in a meaningful way. Sheepdogs understand that society has a higher role in everyone's welfare. Sheepdogs are well aware they face threats from wolves, but often overlooked is the occasional threat from looking after sheep as well.

The threat from wolves is quite obvious: wolves are ruthless, apathetic, and selfish. If you are a sheepdog, your natural instinct is to protect others. But sheep also pose a threat to sheepdogs because they can prey on their innate empathy or worse, exploit sympathy. Occasionally becoming overly empathetic, sheepdogs fail to recognize when to walk away when their empathy becomes a threat to their own welfare.

This is often sadly observed in sheepdogs who are supporting loved ones who are struggling with addiction such as gambling or feel trapped in abusive relationships. If empathy becomes sympathy and the sheepdog fails to recognize when it is time to step away for their own welfare, the sheepdog is at risk of being dragged down with the sheep at their own expense.

At the very beginning of their training, lifeguards are taught to always protect themselves first, and at every stage in their efforts to save a drowning person. When a lifeguard swims out into the ocean to save someone, they are taught never to rush close towards the person in need—the drowning person will instinctively jump on the lifeguard to save themselves and both people could drown.

It is the same in life: sheepdogs must always protect themselves first and know when to walk away from the person they are trying to save. The sheepdog becomes weaker by doing too much to save the sheep. As a sheepdog, you must recognize the danger of overcommitting so you can protect the whole flock, even if it is at the expense of one sheep who cannot help itself in some capacity.

It is critical to have the ability to recognize the types of people you will encounter and identify potential risks to your health. This means avoiding getting caught up in what people say and instead, focus on what they do. Oftentimes we will listen excessively, but we will overlook behaviors. Remember: many people will make promises, but how do they actually act? Don't listen to words alone, look at their actions.

Again, no one has exclusively hardwired sheep or sheepdog qualities, we all have tendencies and dominances, especially under stress. It's only with on reflection that we can truly see how we act and respond in situations that we begin to understand ourselves for better and worse.

FORM AUTHENTIC CONNECTIONS THROUGH SHARED VALUES WITH PEOPLE

Concentric Circles

Just like the iconic red-and-white logo of retail giant Target, people revolve around us in a ring-like circle in our everyday lives. Family, loved ones, and very close friends are near to us, inside the closest circle, while those we are less familiar with are on the outside circles.

Sheep and fellow sheepdogs are the people we allow close to us into the inner circle. These are the people in your environment.

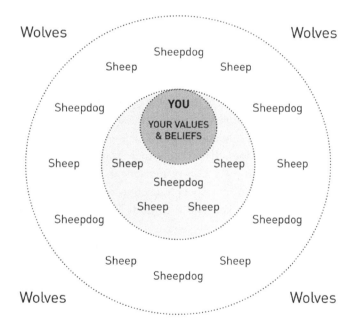

The Sheepdog and its Relationships

We can apply the idea of concentric circles to relationships, too. We are invariably drawn to people who share similar values, because we feel most comfortable around them. Sometimes people get distracted by superficial behaviors that hide people's true values.

We can be entertained by people who don't share our values and we can be intrigued by those who have some redeeming or admirable characteristics, but generally, those who are most aware know they are most comfortable around the people who behave similarly. Sometimes we can be misguided by the groups people associate with and judge them based on their associations, rather than by their independent actions.

"If we are to go forward, we must go back and rediscover those precious values - that all reality hinges on moral foundations and that all reality has spiritual control."

Martin Luther King, Jr.

We enjoy the company of those who share our values. We tend not to even notice the idiosyncrasies of these people, especially in personal and romantic relationships. You know that one quirky thing your partner does that is amusing? Maybe it's a bedtime ritual, a unique laugh, or a fidgety movement. These things may annoy or irritate you in other people, such as work colleagues, but with your close partner, you find them to be cute or funny. This is because of your shared values—you feel aligned with this person and connect with them on a deeper level through trust and understanding.

But these are the very things that annoy you about someone whose values you subliminally or subconsciously find abhorrent. Humans have a subliminal tendency to seek synchronicity, which is why you don't feel comfortable with certain types of extreme personalities—sociopaths and sycophants—but can't put your finger on it or understand quite why.

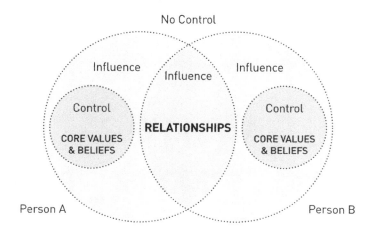

Beliefs, Shared Values & Relationships

While we all have different beliefs or belief systems, our values are the principles or standards of behavior that we consider to be admirable and important. They are the qualities we feel within ourselves and also look for in others.

Values can become virtues (morally good qualities) or vices (immoral behaviors or bad habits). Even if the vices are risky—be it drugs, alcohol, promiscuous behavior or worse—you're more likely to be more at ease with people who share those vices, just as you would be with someone has similar virtues.

"What are the benefits of a Stoic life? I would say, it is an ancient and honorable package of advice on how to stay out of the clutches of those who are trying to get you on the hook, trying to give you a feeling of obligation, trying to get moral leverage on you, to force you to bend to their will."

James Stockdale

YOUR CONTENTMENT DEPENDS ON FIRST BELIEVING THE WORLD IS A GOOD PLACE

Tools for Life

Understanding the three acceptances relating to control, how we approach the world, and how we chose our environment is a crucial step on the road to true success.

We control our reactions and choose how to respond to the world. By focusing on the ability to adapt, we can start to 'control the controllables.' When we recognize those who appear most sheep-like and wolf-like in our lives, we can navigate and control the concentric circles of our relationships. And once we recognize these, we can influence how we approach the world we live in.

Adapt
You only control one thing: Control the controllable

When faced with a setback, you have a choice: react against what you have no control over or control the one thing you can—your perception and response. Do not dwell or stop dead in your tracks. Removing the instinct to respond emotionally is increasingly difficult, but necessary. Accept the facts and circumstances as they are. Starting with your own response and giving yourself the belief that you are in control of the most important thing is one of the simplest and easiest ways we can increase the probability of a favorable outcome.

We don't control most of the things in our life. Therefore, we don't know for sure what will arise—anything can happen. By accepting that as early as possible, you will be able to adapt more quickly. When a shocking event happens, be it positive or negative, the key is to react to it in a positive way, adapt to it and shift your focus away from the event itself. You can always process it later.

Respond
You determine if the world is friendly: Be positive

The physiology of the brain has given us a few common sayings about how humans react: there's fight or flight, and rest or digest. But there's also a freeze. Animals in the wild will freeze with shock when faced with new scenarios that completely overwhelm them. This is something you want to avoid at all costs, because there is no reaction or processing of the event. You must be adaptable to whatever occurs. Don't spend time worrying about what has happened and why. That leads us to the next step, respond positively.

Don't create barriers for your own success. On a psychological level, why would you think negatively about your ability to achieve your goals? There are enough people that are going to try to obstruct you or tell you things that you can't do. You can't control that. But what you can control is what you believe about yourself and the challenges that lie ahead.

Increase Probability
Environment matters more than genes: Give yourself the best chance

Increasing probability means making smart choices and putting yourself in the best position to be happy and successful. There's a saying: "Sit outside a barbershop long enough and you'll get a haircut." What does this mean?

Associate with the wrong people and you will slowly and unconsciously adopt their behaviors. People forget they have choices. You can move, you can change your job, you can react in a way that you choose, but many forget this. Increase your probability. As motivational speaker Jim Rohn is known for saying:

"You're the average of the five people you spend the most time with."

You can increase the likelihood that you will accomplish your goal by being as prepared as possible, both physically and mentally. Say you have a big meeting or presentation coming up for your job. Going into that office or boardroom, understand that you have to deliver your best, but also know that you do not control how people are going to react.

How you carry yourself, how you dress and how you present yourself when you walk into that room are all important; arming your mind with positive beliefs is equally impactful.

KNOW YOUR CONCENTRIC CIRCLES. KNOW WHO IS IN THEM

Finding your Inner Sheepdog

Societies exist on the basis that we all need each other—and various forms of relationships—to survive and co-exist. This social interdependence allows us all to thrive. As sheepdogs we protect the weak and vulnerable, and these people in turn support us, knowing that we once were young and in need of direction, or will be frail and in need of support. Sheepdogs feel an instinct and duty to ward off wolves.

But sheepdogs must recognize their own personal value and not sacrifice their health for sheep that are either unwilling or unable to make an effort to help themselves. The objective is to help those you can, but never at your own expense. There is also a greater duty to the flock, to society. No one sheep should expose the whole flock to the danger and risk of its demise. And the sheepdog must recognize the duty is always to the collective—society first, individual second.

Values and Circles

As we journey through life we encounter many wolves and sheep. Be aware of your concentric circles and who you let through to your most inner circle. Never discount people and never prejudge, but base your circles on the actions, not only the words, of the people you trust.

This naturally takes time, experience, and wisdom, but our innate sense of synchronicity with other people's values allows us to find comfort with those who share the same value system.

Life is like a journey by boat in the sea. Aboard you have your loved ones and those who care for each other. You'll need support from fellow travelers in ships for advice and help. You will encounter undesirables on your journey. And finally there will be good weather and there will be storms. How we weather the storms and squalls comes next.

Ideas for Action

- *What worries you or consumes your thoughts the most?*

- *How many of these things are truly in your control?*

- *Do certain people in your life bother or annoy you?*

- *Do you let others exert control over your reactions?*

- *How will you react better to events that occur?*

- *Are you focusing on what you are grateful to have?*

- *Are you choosing to spend time with the right kind of people?*

- *Are you surrounded by sheep, wolves, or sheepdogs?*

- *Who are in your concentric circles?*

- *Are you stacking the deck in your favor?*

Part II

PURPOSE & PASSION

"Faithless to be yourself in a world that is constantly trying to make you something else is the greatest accomplishment."

Ralph Waldo Emerson

Know Thyself

"He who knows others is wise. He who knows himself is enlightened."

Lao Tzu

In the early 1960s, a young boy named Paul Hewson was born to a Protestant mother and a Catholic father in Dublin, Ireland. Paul earned good grades in school from a young age and was popular among his classmates, particularly for his charm and candidness.

But life threw him a curveball when his mother suddenly passed away from a brain hemorrhage, leaving a young boy without direction or purpose. The tragedy threw him spiraling into a state of depression and loneliness.

At his lowest point, just as he was searching for motivation and direction, he found it in the most unlikely place: a note on the bulletin board at his high school, posted by a 14-year-old in search of musicians to assemble a group. Anyone interested was told to report to his house to play some tunes. Five teenagers from the school, including young Paul, showed up.

Not yet a brilliant vocalist, Paul brought his enthusiasm and energy to the new five-piece group, which they named Feedback. Soon after, the band changed their name and Paul Hewson did, too. Feedback became U2, Paul became Bono and thus began the story of one of the most successful bands in modern music.

Bono found identity, purpose, and most of all, happiness in his true passion.

"As a rock star, I have two instincts: I want to have fun, and I want to change the world. I have a chance to do both."

Bono

The Two Most Important Questions

In philosophy, there are countless thought-provoking questions about the world and our role in it, but the two fundamental ones are: "Who am I?" and "Why am I here?" Or, in other words: what is my identity and what is my purpose in life? At some stage in life, everyone is faced with these two questions in some form. Many of us ask these questions only at times of challenge or difficulty.

One of the first steps to discovering your identity and purpose is understanding the values that are important to you. Traditional morality—the basic idea that there is behavior that is right and behavior that is wrong—form the foundation of our identities.

Both Socrates and Plato gave priority to being virtuous over things such as pleasure, power, wealth or materialistic items. In Plato's *Gorgias*, it is suggested that: "it is better to suffer wrong than to do wrong." In other words, doing something that is ethically wrong is more evil or worse than suffering wrong.

In the *Republic*, Plato says that the morally good person enjoys an inner harmony, whereas the wicked person—no matter how rich or powerful—is fundamentally at odds with himself and the world and will never find true inner contentment or harmony.

Most religions and faiths are also based on this conception of morality. A person who obeys the commandments and lives a life according to God's laws will find peace and happiness both in this life and the next.

"Happiness is when what you think, what you say, and what you do are in harmony."

Mahatma Gandhi

KNOW THY AUTHENTIC SELF. DEVELOP AUTHENTIC AWARENESS

Your Superpower: Identity and Purpose

The life story of Nelson Mandela is widely known and often filled with words like hero, inspiration, fighter, leader, and visionary. While he has crossed over into icon status, Mandela was human like the rest of us, and his experiences during his childhood and young adulthood greatly influenced who he became and how he viewed the world.

Mandela was born in 1918 in the rural Eastern Cape in Qunu, South Africa, a village located in a narrow, grassy valley surrounded by mostly treeless land. It was home to a few hundred people who lived in beehive-shaped houses made of mud walls and a wood pole in the center.

As the youngest son of an esteemed African chief, Mandela was immediately immersed in the customs of the Thembu people and, like all children in the village—as Mandela wrote in his 1994 autobiography, *Long Walk to Freedom*—he learned mainly through observation.

"We were meant to learn through imitation and emulation, not through questions," he wrote. "In my household, questions were considered a nuisance; adults imparted information as they considered necessary." Later, Mandela was also influenced by the instruction of his Christian mission school education.

"There is no passion to be found playing small in settling for a life that is less than the one you are capable of living."

Nelson Mandela

Eventually, starting in 1939, Mandela studied at both the University of Fort Hare (an institution for black South Africans) and the University of Witwatersrand, where he first saw the politics of African nationalism.

In establishing a law practice in Johannesburg with a friend, Mandela witnessed more injustices that opposed his moral upbringing and continued to impact him. Knowing even these simple details of Mandela's childhood and background make it easy to understand who he was as a leader and how he came to know his identity and find his purpose in life.

"Mandela's heroism is the heroism of a man who suffered so badly for what he thought of as freedom. And yet when he had the upper hand, he has this incredible self-control and these incredible leadership qualities."

Bono

How do you answer the question, "Who am I?" How do you know what your identity is? Broadly, identity refers to how you recognize yourself. When people struggle with the question, I often ask, in a joking way: What is your superpower? What are you really good at? What is the one thing you do that impacts others?

Mandela, for example, recognized that he was equipped to struggle for the freedom of his people, and his political involvement carried out this understanding.

Identity is your internal image, as opposed to an external image, or how others see you. Your external image is made up of what people see on the outside—this is what most people in the world define you by based on incomplete information.

Introverted, gentle, and always wearing those black-rimmed glasses, Clark Kent and his personality traits constitute the external image others see in everyday life. But of course, Clark Kent's internal image is the extraordinary and valiant Superman.

People you encounter will often evaluate you based on outward traits, your appearance, the color of your skin, ethnicity, sexual orientation, or social status. Some will create an external image based on actions, behavior, religious views, and more. But none of this matters. Only your identity—your internal image—can truly impact your life and happiness.

Many high achievers I've worked with initially struggled to know who they are and what their purpose and passion was. Rather than approaching it from a deep philosophical perspective, I like to ask: *What is your superhero power and what would you do with it?*

The answers are illuminating. Many realize they have gifts of communication, compassion, conviction, a desire to help others, do good, and inspire colleagues and friends. Just like any superhero, you have skills and gifts that direct your purpose and identity.

Our identity originates from our belief system which is a product of our upbringing, our faith and our family members. In Mandela's case, he was very much influenced by the customs and traditions of the Thembu people. Like the foundation of a house, these ideas are fixed and instilled from birth—it is very difficult to change them.

"On a deeper level you are already complete. When you realize that, there is a playful, joyous energy behind what you do."

Eckhart Tolle

YOUR WHY, YOUR PURPOSE IS YOUR REASON FOR EVERYTHING

You Are Not Your Job

The mistake most people make when considering identity is deferring to their occupation as a starting point for explaining who they are. Saying, "I am a doctor" or "I am a financial advisor" or "I am business owner" or "I am a teacher" is how most will begin to define themselves as individuals.

Relatedly, one's career is often directly related to economic status and it also influences leisure activities and relationships, all of which can shape one's identity. But identity is not who you are professionally—it is much more fundamental than that. People who strongly associate themselves with their career and then suddenly lose their job will find this out fast.

Identity is who you are as a person, your strengths, passions, abilities, talents and vulnerabilities. Identity is a combination of both positive and negative traits.

"If one does not know to which port one is sailing, no wind is favorable."

Seneca

Know Your Why

The decisions we make are fundamentally influenced and inspired by what we view as our purpose in life. In its most basic definition, purpose is the reason for which something is done or for which something exists. If making money is your sole focus, day in and day out, that's your purpose—and it's your choice, no one else's. In a larger context, it is what you understand your role and relationship with the world to be.

For the individual, purpose inspires one's vision in life, his or her overall goals on a wider scale and a responsibility that one feels the need to fulfill. These objectives create meaning and drive us to do what we do each day. Simply put, purpose is our internal, self-generated compass that provides a sense of direction and helps guide goals and behaviors.

The greatest advantage that comes from knowing your identity and purpose is that your work-life balance is no longer an issue. In this circumstance, work and life have a completely different importance—work is a subset of life, not an addition.

How do you find your true purpose? For most of us, our purpose lies in our responsibilities to others, including our family, community, and friends. For others, or for some periods of our life, one's purpose can be professional or vocation based. On the other hand, one's purpose can also be clouded by society, outside or peer influences and material things.

When thinking about identity, it is important to remember that there usually isn't a simple or sudden event that helps a person identify who they are and what their role in life is. Most tend to search for one moment that will lead to discovery; however, it is the journey over time that often reveals true identity and purpose.

"Everyone has his own specific vocation or mission in life; everyone must carry out a concrete assignment that demands fulfillment. Therein he cannot be replaced, nor can his life be repeated. Thus, everyone's task is unique as is his specific opportunity to implement it."

Viktor E. Frankl

I HATE TO BREAK IT TO YOU. YOU ARE NOT YOUR JOB

Realizing Your Passion And Purpose

Oftentimes, realizing your true identity and purpose in life may not be apparent right away. Sometimes it can take years for you to recognize it. This is what happened to a well-known NFL player for the San Francisco 49ers I was fortunate to coach. His name? Chris Borland.

Growing up in Kettering, Ohio, Borland was driven by athletics for most of his youth, becoming a letterman in football, track, basketball, and tennis at Archbishop Alter High School. Sports helped him strive towards a greater goal. Ultimately, he was recruited for football and chose to attend Wisconsin. Later, he was drafted in the third round of the NFL Draft by the San Francisco 49ers.

I crossed paths with Borland during my time with the 49ers as the director of elite performance. Straightaway from our first encounter, I could tell he was a little bit different than some of the other players. Borland was very serious about his profession, He was a pro football player and he was going to do everything in his power to be the best he could be at his position.

From nutrition to training, Borland was zeroed in from the start and he would constantly ask me to review his recovery protocols, diet, supplements, and what he was doing on his time off. Borland was a rookie, but he didn't act like one. He was always searching for ways to improve.

During his first season in the league, Borland was called up to a starting position after Pro Bowl starting linebacker Patrick Willis was placed on injured reserve with a toe injury, and the rookie instantly delivered. Borland earned all-rookie honors for recording 107 tackles, a sack, two interceptions, and a fumble recovery.

But towards the end of the season, he approached me at dinner one night and asked me about the book, *League of Denial: The NFL's Concussion Crisis*, written by two San Francisco-based brothers,

Mark Fainaru-Wada and Steve Fainaru. I had read it, but I wondered why he would, especially at this point in his career.

What I did not know at the time was that he had already sustained two diagnosed concussions during his athletic career, plus a dozen more that he did not report. After learning about the perils of repeated brain trauma and the degenerative brain disease chronic traumatic encephalopathy (CTE), Borland announced his retirement from professional football in March 2015.

Chris had discovered a new purpose—his role was no longer to play the game, but to educate and advocate for player safety and share insight from his decision and personal experience with brain injuries.

Just like Borland, Colin Kaepernick—another great person I was fortunate to know and work with—realized his identity, and along with Eric Reid, expressed his purpose. Through this, Kaepernick became the face of a new civil rights movement—and a powerful Nike ad—after his National Anthem protests and subsequent departure from the league.

And even though she is still playing tennis, Serena Williams—one of the greatest athletes, male or female, in any sport—is becoming more socially active and embracing a new role model status as a working woman who is also balancing motherhood.

"We don't stop playing because we grow old; we grow old because we stop playing."

George Bernard Shaw

These are athletes who have discovered a purpose beyond sport and their personal identity. Your purpose guides your behavior, attitudes, and your life decisions. When people become consciously aware of what's motivating them to think and act as they are, they can develop a clear understanding of personal goals and intentions. And that will help define one's identity.

As part of embracing this new role, Borland now works with After the Impact Fund, a non-profit organization that assists former NFL players and military veterans who suffer from traumatic injuries. The program provides a support network and gives these men and women a renewed sense of purpose. Funny how it all works out, isn't it?

Most of the time, people are taught how to develop a positive identity so they can self-actualize their potential as a human being. But in today's world, the modern dilemma for many is that the external factors—beauty, physical appearance, clothes, cars, and other materialistic items, that are now amplified and glorified through social media—are often regarded as characteristics that define identity.

People who identify with a social media personality can adopt their tendencies, and that becomes their purpose. And those who are confused about their identity and purpose are the most susceptible to misdirection and disillusionment through cults and other organizations.

"He who has a why to live for can bear almost any how."

Friedrich Nietzsche

But What About the Opinions of Others?

Oftentimes, we become overly concerned about what others think. This isn't necessarily a bad thing, but sometimes we worry about the opinions of people whose opinion shouldn't matter.

Let me give you an example: you are walking down the street after getting a new haircut. On your way out, a random person makes a comment about your hair. Then, another stranger—a bald man—says something about it, too. When you get in the car, a family member remarks on your haircut as well.

Which opinion would you think about the most when you get home? Many times, it's the comment from a random stranger or a person with a terrible haircut themselves that will have the most impact, rather than the opinion of a close friend or family member.

"I will not let anyone walk through my mind with their dirty feet."

Mahatma Gandhi

Before you consider the value of an opinion, first consider who it's coming from and consider his or her importance or relevance. Far too often, people pass negative comments on us, but they are only doing so in order to drag you down to their level.

In the vast majority of cases, the negative comment is likely coming from a place of jealousy or insecurity. On the other hand, the opinions of those who really care and love us should be given real value, especially when they have the courage to tell us things that may be uncomfortable. After all, this is what true friends do.

What about when people comment on decisions or mistakes that we make? Consider that many times, the person making the comment isn't exactly in the best position themselves to make an observation. "He that is without sin among you, let him first cast a stone."

Then consider the mistakes of the other person. In the 1934 movie, *It's a Gift*, W. C. Fields' character is accused of being drunk and he responds, "Yeah, and you're crazy. But I'll be sober tomorrow and you'll be crazy the rest of your life."

Very often, the person that is judging you for a temporary error—something you can get over—is an individual who has made a fatal, long-term error they cannot get over. Every opinion matters, but some matter more than others and it's important to think about this when interacting with other people. Minor mistakes will be long forgotten, while those often judging you leave trails of permanent damage behind them.

We often get fooled by the projected image others want you to see. We need to realize that our problems may seem like the most terrible in the world, but most of the time we lose perspective. We look at others and think they have a perfect life, but in reality, their situation could be far worse than anything you are dealing with.

This usually comes down to two things: a fear of being vulnerable and judged as imperfect, and an attempt to project a public image they want their neighbors, coworkers, and peers to assume is reality. But no one is perfect and no one has a perfect life.

Your neighbor with the 'perfect life' has a marriage that is barely functioning. Or the successful professional is cheating on his wife; the executive has a secret drug addiction. Or the seemingly dynamic CEO who is on the verge of a series of irreversible medical issues from years of an extremely stressful lifestyle. The bottom line is you simply don't know the stresses and challenges of others.

I often tell high achievers who feel overwhelmed and constantly compare themselves to others to refocus with this short activity.

Try it yourself. Take a moment and imagine all the 'more successful' people you are comparing yourself to are in one room. Everyone is seated in a circle, chatting and telling each other of the great accomplishments or projects they are working on. After a while you are each given a blank piece of paper and pen.

Everyone is asked to write down the biggest private issue they carry with them every day or the greatest burden they are dealing with at that moment. When everyone is finished they crumple up their piece of paper and throw it into the center of the circle. You can swap with anyone, have their wealth and health, however first you must pick up their piece of paper and take that problem also.

I assure you, when you pick up some of the other private issues people are dealing with, you'll be looking for your own piece of paper back.

Keep these three stories in your mind next time you begin to experience feelings of inadequacy.

"Don't let the noise of others' opinions drown out your own inner voice."

Steve Jobs

ARTIFACTS AND BEHAVIORS ARE YOUR VALUES MANIFESTED

The Iceberg Model

What about those who seem to have their identity figured out because of their careers, be it a business owner or CEO? High achievers who only identify in professional terms eventually struggle to find true harmony and balance in their life and fail to achieve long-term contentment.

Many times, those who encounter what is an identity crisis end up becoming confused with their true purpose in life. The result often ends in searching for purpose, distractions or thrills which end up becoming addictions, whether it's hoarding, gambling, drug abuse, promiscuity or alcohol.

Everyone benefits from a personal purpose and identity. When it is all put together, we can arrive at a place of contentment with ourselves and synchronicity with others—think long-term happiness, job satisfaction and a healthy personal balance.

So who are you? How do you think? What forms your thought processes and inclinations? This is obviously a very complex series of questions, but I've used a specific model to help high achievers understand how they think—and how to appreciate how others think and act—so we can be more understanding of the nature of people we meet and deal with.

To begin to understand this model we need to think of each other as icebergs. We see and interact with people's behaviors, demeanors, appearance—this is what we see above the water line. But these behaviors and appearances are formulated by a series of other more complex interactions below the surface that we must consider so we can appreciate each other fully.

"The greatest fear that human beings experience is not death, which is inevitable, but consideration of the distinct possibility of living a worthless life."

Kilroy J. Oldster

LEAD WITH VALUES, AND BEHAVIORS TAKE CARE OF THEMSELVES

The Belief Bedrock

Our beliefs make up the base of the iceberg, hidden deep underneath the water's surface. Beliefs are essentially what we know to be true. Beliefs can be as simple and systematic as mathematical principles. Beliefs can also originate from faith—for example, if you believe in Christianity, you may believe in some kind of life after death and, thus, in the idea that what you do here will impact that. But they also come from a person's life experiences, upbringing, education, and mentoring.

OBSERVABLE

APPEARANCE
Tangible, overt identifiable
characteristic of a person

BEHAVIOR
Action, outcome or
expression of attitude

UNOBSERVABLE

ATTITUDE
Learned predisposed response to
a person, place or experience

VALUES
An ideal, principle believed to
be correct or morally proper

BELIEF
A fundamental understanding a
person holds to be true to them

The Iceberg Model

Beliefs are informed by your understanding of ethos and ethics. Each individual has his or her own understanding of ethics. Most people learn these moral principles through family and upbringing, religious instruction, peer influences, popular culture, and social interactions. Ethics—from the ancient Greek words 'ethikos' and 'ethos,' meaning relating to one's character—are guidelines for conduct. An ethical character is described as one of honesty, fairness, equality and dignity.

"Parents who discipline their child by discussing the consequences of their actions produce children who have better moral development, compared to children whose parents use authoritarian methods and punishment."

Simon Baron-Cohen

Unfortunately in today's society, we have more and more people who don't have role models and a stable environment that can establish a belief system and ethical understanding from a young age. It's like trying to build a home on quicksand. If the ground is unstable and wobbly, how can you expect to construct something that is well balanced and secure?

Both ethics and our character are formed from moral instruction guided from the very beginning of our life. A person's ethics affects a person's general set of values. Each of us expresses those values through behaviors and actions.

While some people adopt a set of beliefs and ethics during their childhood, others find grounding elsewhere. This is why many turn to organizations, like the United States Marine Corps, which provides a belief system—and in turn, values, identity, and purpose —for young men and women who have struggled to find an established environment that can provide that for them.

"The culture of a workplace—an organization's values, norms and practices—has a huge impact on our happiness and success."

Adam Grant

GREAT LEADERS ENCOURAGE INDIVIDUALITY

Values and Attitudes

Simply defined, values are the basic beliefs that guide or motivate attitudes or actions. Sitting on top of what we know to be true, values are the ideals or standards that people use to direct their behavior. They are what people strive to realize in their lives.

How do we make decisions about what is important in life and about what is right or wrong in human behavior? By using our values as the standards by which we judge these things.

The Marine Corps serves as a clear picture and practical example of a set of values. While there are other common and important values, there are three specific ones that define how every Marine in the Corps thinks, acts and fights: honor, courage and commitment.

Honor: *"The quality that empowers Marines to exemplify the ultimate in ethical and moral behavior: to never lie, cheat, or steal; to abide by an uncompromising code of integrity; to respect human dignity; and to have respect and concern for each other. Maturity, dedication, trust, and dependability."*

Courage: *"The mental, moral, and physical strength...to do what is right, to adhere to a higher standard of personal conduct, to lead by example, and to make tough decisions under stress and pressure."*

Commitment: *"This is the spirit of determination and dedication within members... it promotes the highest order of discipline for unit and self... it's an unrelenting determination to achieve a standard of excellence in every endeavor."*

Both individuals and organizations have values. One of the easiest ways to understand and realize your values is to notice how you feel around an individual or specific company or group of people. Do you feel uneasy? Do you find yourself subconsciously awkward, tense or embarrassed while around a particular group? If so, it's usually a sign that your value system does not align with the rest of the crowd.

On the other hand, if you feel comfortable or calm, especially over a long period of time, it is likely because you have similar values as the people around you.

Just as the Marine Corps established its three key values of honor, courage, and commitment, most companies also institute some sort of value system that they promote and talk about with employees. One that works exceptionally well that I've seen firsthand is the system at WD-40.

Yes, we're talking about that classic blue-and-yellow can with the red top that's likely sitting in your garage. That signature lubricant oil is just one of the household products that the $408 million, 450-employee company manufactures out of its San Diego, Calif.-based headquarters, led by CEO Garry Ridge. While the product is good, it's the values system that Ridge has created that makes the company an exemplary one.

When I arrived at the San Diego headquarters building to meet Ridge for the first time, I mistakenly tried to enter through a side door instead of the main entrance. How did I know it was a side entry? Written on the door in big letters was: FOR TRIBE MEMBERS ONLY. The main door had no such sign.

This is one of the most interesting aspects of WD-40: the employees describe themselves as a tribe, not a company. This is the initial step in instituting the system that Ridge has created. The second step involves clearly explaining the values of the system.

At the headquarters, the values are not only framed on a wall in a hallway for all to see. They are plainly outlined so that the employees can find 'kindred spirits' and have the freedom to make autonomous decisions while still acting as one. Because there are many interpretations for different values, offering examples instead of simple definitions is an important step.

GREAT TEAMS HAVE A CLEAR AND SHARED VISION

In speaking with people around the headquarters during my visit, I learned of another way that Ridge leads his team according to the company's values. As WD-40 was redesigning the offices in San Diego, architects often brought Ridge updated plans for his approval. But each time they presented the new layouts, Ridge noticed that they made his office larger than the other offices in the space—this was not in line with his original instructions.

Before the renovation, Ridge specified that every office should be the exact same size. How's that for humility? Ridge's actions are directly related to the fourth value in the WD-40 list: succeeding as a tribe while excelling as an individual.

WD-40 Values

We value doing the right thing.

We value creating positive, lasting memories in all our relationships.

We value making it better than it is today.

We value succeeding as a tribe while excelling as individuals.

We value owning it and passionately acting on it.

We value sustaining the WD-40 Company economy.

Ridge also outlines these ideas in his book, *Helping People Win at Work: A Business Philosophy Called "Don't Mark My Paper, Help Me Get an A"*, written with prominent author and management expert, Ken Blanchard. While the values above are specific to Ridge and WD-40, there are others that are recognized as common values throughout the world:

Love: You must show respect and demonstrate kindness towards others and appreciate who they are as individuals. Keep other people's input in high regard and care for them and those that are important to them. In the context of a leader, this allows individuals on your staff to work for you while knowing that the things they care about most are looked after.

Honesty: Good character means being loyal and free of deceit and untruthfulness. No matter how unpopular or unwelcome an issue might be, it's important to always be truthful and transparent with others. Honesty is directly related to trust and those who are trusted are seen as dependable leaders.

Fairness: Always strive to be fair and just. You should not be biased—you must treat everyone equally, especially in a leadership position. Of course, this means living without discrimination based on gender, sexuality, ethnicity, etc.

Freedom: It is important to encourage freedom of thought with others, so they are able to take initiative. This demonstrates trust and appreciation and allows for improvement, innovative ideas and development for all parties involved.

Unity: Foster a sense of community and team spirit among a group, be it colleagues, family members or friends. Recognize your role is bigger than just you—this means focusing on more than just personal goals. For those in a leadership position, efforts to achieve goals that benefit the entire organization lead to sustained success.

Tolerance: Be open minded, kind and act in a manner that is always beneficial to each staff member and the team as a whole.

Responsibility: Be accountable for your actions in every situation. Irresponsibility undermines cooperation, collaboration and constructive social relationships.

Respect: Demonstrate respect and admiration for others' abilities, qualities and achievements. This can be as simple as listening to others and valuing contributions. Be compassionate and generous with your time.

"One of the most beautiful qualities of true friendship is to understand and to be understood."

Seneca

As you establish values, they will dictate how your mind operates and ultimately, what your attitude is towards others. An attitude is a reaction based on our value system and how we see the world. We have attitudes to everything—they are instinctual responses, often based on emotional attachments to various memories or recollections. Your attitude is subconscious— sometimes you don't even notice your facial reaction to events or people. Most importantly, attitudes direct your behaviors.

Artifacts and Behaviors

When we go on vacation or visit a new place or city, we notice the unfamiliar around us. Upon entering a gift shop, you may look around and browse the tables and shelves, or maybe engage in conversation with one of the store's clerks. Upon checking in your hotel room for the weekend, you might explore the lobby or restaurant area, or sit on the bed to test out how comfy it is.

When you arrive home and tell someone where you were, they might ask you, "Oh! What was it like?" You will describe your experience. Invariably, the description of the experience will be formed by two things: artifacts and behaviors. Artifacts refer to appearances of people and things—how it looked and how it appeared. Behaviors refer to how people treated you and interacted with you.

Take a look back at how the Marines and the WD-40 employees approach values. They know that values are the basis for one's mindset but understand that an explanation alone is not enough. In each case, they go beyond a simple definition and describe what the attitude and behavior of the value means in action and in practice.

"Enlightened leadership is spiritual if we understand spirituality not as some kind of religious dogma or ideology but as the domain of awareness where we experience values like truth, goodness, beauty, love and compassion, and also intuition, creativity, insight and focused attention."

Deepak Chopra

The Culture of People

Artifacts and behaviors are the elements of culture we see when we experience groups of people. Was the store clerk friendly towards you or annoyed when you asked a question about an item? Was your hotel room clean and tidy or was trash still there from a previous guest? This is directly related to the idea that culture is like an iceberg.

When we see an iceberg, we only see the portion that is visible above the water—this is the tip of the iceberg. Similarly, when you visit somewhere, you see the cleanliness of the room or the color of the couch at a friend's house, or the way the person at the front desk treated you. But in reality, that tip of the iceberg is only a small piece of a much larger mass that extends deep down under the water, farther than the eye can see.

When we talk about this in relation to culture, it means that the artifacts and behaviors are only a small part of the components that make up culture. You're exposed to the tip of the iceberg, but you have to understand that those things are based on far more substantial things. Hiding beneath the water's surface are deeper, more complex ideas known as beliefs, attitudes, and values.

"A people that values its privileges above its principles soon loses both."

Dwight D. Eisenhower

CULTURE

Environment a person is most frequently
physically and psychologically exposed to

OBSERVABLE

APPEARANCE

Tangible, overt identifiable
characteristic of a person

BEHAVIOR

Action, outcome or
expression of attitude

The Culture Model

Culture can be viewed as an iceberg, but the same concept applies when dealing with people. When we meet people initially, our first reaction is based on how they act towards us and how they treat us. We are influenced by their appearance and their mannerisms, but the longer we spend with people, the more we become aware of their attitudes.

How are attitudes developed and defined? Attitudes are how we think about things or people. They are influenced by values, virtues and vices, which are all ultimately based on our belief system.

"If you want the cooperation of humans around you, you must make them feel they are important, and you do that by being genuine and humble."

Nelson Mandela

The most classic example of a sports organization with strong cultural values is the All Blacks, the New Zealand national rugby team. Even if you aren't familiar with the team or the sport, there are lessons to be learned from one of the most successful sporting teams ever—a team that also took a rapid downturn and, as a result, completely rebuilt the culture of the club.

The principles of the All Blacks culture were focused on individual character and personal leadership. One of the first and foremost rules is: *better people make better All Blacks*—there's a 'no dickheads' policy. The team emphasizes honesty and authenticity, and people who "keep it real" and are true to themselves. And similar to WD-40's values, the All Blacks also promote individual commitment to a group effort—meaning that no one is bigger than the team and everyone must connect towards a common goal.

One of the most prevalent examples in the modern-day business world is the corporate culture at Apple Inc. Though the tech giant is known for both positive and negative aspects of culture, the company's leadership through Steve Jobs, and now, Tim Cook, has focused on a high-level of innovation, creativity, and a best-of-the-best approach among employees. Apple's management motivates and encourages its employees to develop new ideas, methods, and products, which enables the company to stay competitive and deliver to customer needs.

When a group of people—even from different backgrounds and belief systems—connect on values, it becomes the common language of a group's culture. Values are what will create synchronicity and that feeling of being comfortable within a group or organization. It's like how the good guys in the superhero movies usually stick together, while the bad guys are left on the outside in their own group. People tend to feel the most comfortable with those who have a similar set of beliefs and values.

So what's your superpower? If you were given the choice to select your special abilities, what would you do with your life? What values are most important to you?

"It is what we make out of what we have, not what we are given, that separates one person from another."

Nelson Mandela

Ideas for Action

- *Ask yourself this simple question: "Who am I?"*

- *What are my strengths, my positive qualities?*

- *What are my limitations and biases? What are my opportunities for improvement?*

- *What do others see as my greatest gifts to them?*

- *Do I truly recognize my gifts and strengths as a person, not as a professional?*

- *Why am I here? What is my purpose in life?*

- *What makes me passionate? What makes me truly upset?*

- *What are my superpowers? Do I use these gifts properly?*

- *Can I distinguish my profession from who I am as a person?*

- *Do I judge on values or on beliefs?*

- *Does my group connect on a deep or superficial level?*

- *Do I see the values and qualities of others?*

- *Do I make superficial judgements on behaviors or appearance?*

- *How do my behaviors reflect my values?*

- *Can I explain my values as a person clearly as actions for someone?*

Part III

THE HOLISTIC HUMAN

"I am not worried if scientists go and explain everything. This is for a very simple reason: an impala sprinting across the Savannah can be reduced to biomechanics, and Bach can be reduced to counterpoint, yet that does not decrease one iota our ability to shiver as we experience impalas leaping or Bach thundering.

We can only gain and grow with each discovery that there is structure underlying the most accessible levels of things that fill us with awe.

But there is an even stronger reason why I am not afraid that scientists will inadvertently go and explain everything--it will never happen. While in certain realms, it may prove to be the case that science can explain anything, it will never explain everything.

As should be obvious after all these pages, as part of the scientific process, for every question answered, a dozen newer ones are generated. And they are usually far more puzzling, more challenging than the prior problems.

This was stated wonderfully in a quote by a geneticist named Haldane earlier in the century: 'Life is not only stranger than we imagine, it is stranger than we can imagine.' We will never have our flames extinguished by knowledge. The purpose of science is not to cure us of our sense of mystery and wonder, but to constantly reinvent and reinvigorate it."

Robert M. Sapolsky

The Trouble with Testosterone and Other Essays
on the Biology of the Human Predicament

Descarte's Error

"I think, therefore I am."

René Descartes

There is arguably no saying more famous in philosophy than this phrase by French philosopher and mathematician René Descartes. In this expression—known famously in Latin as *Cogito, ergo sum*—Descartes is essentially suggesting that we control our own thoughts by simply thinking something. In other words, the mind controls itself and is separate from the body physically.

Born March 31, 1596, Descartes was one of the first to challenge traditional Aristotelian thinking with his thesis about the distinct relationship between the mind and body—an idea we now call mind-body dualism.

In Descartes' *Meditations*, he argues that the mind is a thinking, non-extended substance that engages in things like rational thought, desires, feeling, and visualizing; while the body is a non-thinking, extended substance that is related to space. He believed that the mind is something completely different and separate from the body, and therefore it is possible for one to exist without the other.

"If I had to define a major depression in a single sentence, I would describe it as a "genetic/neuro-chemical disorder requiring a strong environmental trigger whose characteristic manifestation is an inability to appreciate sunsets."

Robert M. Sapolsky

This idea—known as the mind-body problem—is still debated today. How do the mind and body interact if they are distinct and different? For example, how can the mind cause our body to move, like when you reach out to shake someone's hand when you meet them? On the other hand, how can the body cause feelings and emotions?

I've got news for you: Descartes was wrong. There is no distinct separation between the mind and the body. Neurologist Antonio Damasio explores this idea in depth in his 1994 book, *Descartes' Error: Emotion, Reason, and the Human Brain*, in which he discusses how emotions guide behavior and decision-making. Like with genetics and epigenetics, the more we learned from science about neurology and physiology the more we started to understand how our mind and body interacted.

Psychology is simply just unsolved physiology, something we don't quite understand fully yet but are learning about at a rapid pace. There is no separation between psychology and physiology—in truth, it really should be referred to as psychophysiology.

Our brain and body are linked together, and we can influence both by each other. There are a whole series of neuro-chemicals and neuro-hormones that influence how we think and act. It's a two-way street. In other words, we can think in a positive way and affect our physiology as well.

"Typically, people who exercise, start eating better and becoming more productive at work. They smoke less and show more patience with colleagues and family. They use their credit cards less frequently and say they feel less stressed. Exercise is a keystone habit that triggers widespread change."

Charles Duhigg

Health is the basis for all success. This is all based on the fundamental idea of *Mens sana in corpore sano*, a Latin phrase that is usually translated to 'a healthy mind in a healthy body.' What does this mean? Simply: a healthy lifestyle will influence our mind in a positive way. If you are eating fruits and vegetables and healthy food; getting fresh air and natural sunlight; surrounding yourself with positive people; and exercising your body and muscles, you will impact your psychological well-being in a beneficial way.

This goes back to one of the first Laws of Life that we discussed: we become our environment. The people we are surrounded by and the environment we live in can have an influence on us, both positively and negatively. The food we eat and the activities and things we do with our body will influence our mind and mental state, and vice versa, as our mind can also affect our physical qualities and condition.

HUMANS
ARE
COMPLEX
ADAPTIVE
ORGANISMS

The TTPP Model

After seeing first-hand how elite performers in the NFL, NBA, MLB, professional soccer, and special forces operated in their respective areas, I had to develop a model to help coaches and leaders understand that the mind and body are connected and influence each other.

The methodology I created was designed to promote long, sustainable careers. Far too often, people become caught up in measuring physical outputs and fail to recognize and value holistic performance. This same model—the Tactico-Technical Psycho-Physiological Model—is just as relevant to you as it is to any athlete or military leader.

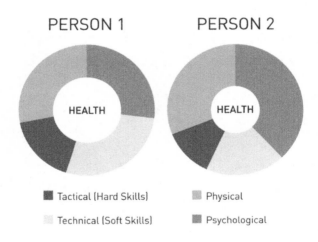

PERSON 1   PERSON 2

HEALTH   HEALTH

■ Tactical (Hard Skills)   Physical
  Technical (Soft Skills)   ■ Psychological

Profiling Compensation and Characteristics of High Achievers

In sports, in business, and in life, health is always at the core of any long-term success. Remember, I am interested in the sustainable success of resilient people, not short-term, sudden gains with the risk of burnout or failure. I want to make better people, not simply make people better.

"Health is a state of complete physical, mental and social well-being and not merely the absence of disease or infirmity."

World Health Organization

We have established that our mental and physical wellness is determined and influenced by both the mind and the body. The next step is understanding the four areas that make up everyone's identity that allow us to succeed, both professionally and personally. The areas are tactical, technical, physiological, and psychological. You cannot assess these four areas unless there's a solid foundation of overall health and well-being.

Technical: This is our soft skill-set; our immediate knowledge and abilities. It can refer to the day-to-day skills that you perform, whether it is in accounting, marketing, or any other fields of work. It can be your interpersonal skills meeting people and developing relationships, or technical organization and analytical skills. In sport, it's the ability to perform a skill in context.

Tactical: This pertains to our hard skills, our experience, wisdom, decision-making, and strategy skills, and how we apply the technical skills in our environment. This is the platform for technical ability, the context in which our skills can be applied. We can be excellent at a skill, but the experience, location, and timing are what will determine its effectiveness, such as having great communication skills, but limited to only one domain or only in one environment.

Physiological: This pertains to our physical abilities and biomechanics, such as strength, endurance, and flexibility, and our overall nutrition and energy systems. Can you execute the skill often or only once? Can you sustain the quality or do you fatigue quickly?

Psychological: This is the control of our emotion, concentration, and state of mind. It's also related to self-belief and how we mentally focus. This is often about the ability to perform under stress and pressure. Can you manage emotions and process information? How do you learn? What is your moral and ethical code as a person?

The Mind Model

In dealing with elite performers in sport, there are many different types of psychological profiling tests that can be used to determine personality traits or behavioral style. The Myers–Briggs Type Indicator and DISC assessment are two examples. These are all excellent assessments, but unless we look at the holistic person, we don't fully grasp the influence of physiology on our psychology. Hence the need to present the integrated model.

In helping identify the issues at hand and in understanding why people fail under pressure or in moments of high stress, I use a three-part mind model that breaks down the psychological domain into three categories: cognitive, spiritual, and emotional.

"Genes are rarely about inevitability, especially when it comes to humans, the brain, or behavior. They're about vulnerability, propensities, tendencies."

Robert M. Sapolsky

These elements help us develop strategies for understanding how we deal with life's challenges. I use this model with CEOs to help demonstrate where limitations are in relation to performance.

Spiritual: This refers to relationships and one's place in the larger world. How does one interact or relate to other people? What is one's mindset in a social setting? This reflects our social interactions. But you can't interpret social behaviors unless you understand yourself first.

Emotional: This relates to how one manages or deals with various events and the degree to which one controls reactions to situations or people. Is there a good understanding of what one controls and what one does not control? Do minor or trivial things easily cause agitation? How do you perceive stress and pressure in different situations?

Cognitive: This refers to how information is processed and how one learns, listens and communicates, specifically related to verbal, visual, or auditory cues. Does one prefer to communicate through diagrams or kinesthetic movements with the arms or hands? How do you think? What pathways do you use to come to conclusions?

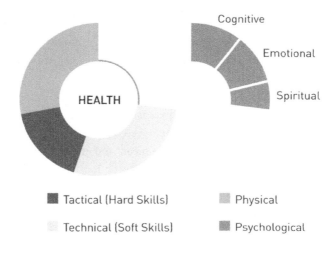

The Psychological Profile

The cognitive, spiritual, and emotional model is an integrated model, not a segmented one, because as we've learned, your physiology can influence well-being, emotional control, and the ability to concentrate. Using these three areas can help us profile elite performers or ourselves and identify how we manage the psychological mind.

While I list different sections and elements, you must understand that all of these are intertwined. We cannot look at the person or leader as a series of parts. The whole is greater than the sum. This is not a reductionist model; humans are not machines.

One of the greatest errors we see in modern society is the influence technology has had on our thinking. We adopt plug-and-play mindsets that we bring with us when dealing with everyday issues. A person is much greater and more complex than that. We are integrated beings—everything affects everything.

When we are using this model to understand others or ourselves, it is important to note that although we can have a predisposition to a particular learning style—i.e., someone who prefers to communicate through drawing diagrams vs. talking—we can also acquire and absorb new ways. For example, someone who is a kinesthetic learner can still acquire the skills to become more analytical in terms of processing.

When I was working with the San Francisco 49ers, it was easy to see that, from a cognitive perspective, running back Frank Gore was a kinesthetic learner. He loved to do things. He required movement to learn, whether that meant moving his hands or feet or jumping right in to try a new move or footwork drill. That was really his best way of learning on the field and it worked for him, but that doesn't mean he doesn't have the ability to inherit or take on a new learning style.

After spending time working with many of them, it is very clear that the men and women in the U.S. Special Forces have and need a strong spiritual psychological perspective for long term success. In observing them using the mind model above, I have noticed that they have a very good sense of community, a good social network of people around them and a strong culture within the group that they rely on. But even in this community there are challenges, especially after they retire or move to other roles in society.

We can also observe ourselves with this mind model by asking similar questions: How do we process information? How do we learn? How do we manage our emotions? Do we communicate well with others? Do we find ourselves more aloof with others? This helps profile our own ability to understand our own mind.

However, here's one of the most interesting aspects of the mind model: many people who function extremely well and efficiently when under pressure in their chosen field actually struggle in what we can call 'normal life.' When the pressure is off, their mind functions in a completely different manner. We often see this with military personnel and surgeons. Context matters.

FOUNDATIONS OF PSYCHOLOGICAL WELLNESS INFLUENCE OUR BELIEF SYSTEM

The Five Foundations of Psychological Wellness

Over the years working with these elite performers, I've seen a lot of trends with the types of issues that arise. Many of these performers start their career from a very early age and get little exposure to normal life. Young prodigies in sport are recruited earlier and earlier; operators in elite units also start training as an adolescent.

Often, this is one of the foundational reasons why they struggle to adapt to societal norms when they leave the theater of operations and remove the stress and pressure they are inoculated to through training and experience. This is not confined to players—coaches are also getting into the business earlier and earlier, often after short playing careers. And again, they have limited or no experience of the wider world and human behaviors.

"A large percentage of what we think of when we talk about stress-related diseases are disorders of excessive stress-responses."

Robert M. Sapolsky

FOUNDATIONS OF WELLBEING

MATURITY

Sophistication, problem solving, education, streetwise intelligence

LIFESTYLE

Life skills, living situation, community, environment

SELF-ESTEEM

Self view, confidence, self respect, addictions, substance use ,abuse

SECURITY

Professional, financial, concerns, fears, demands, public status

ATTACHMENT

Emotional support, tribe, community, relationships, love, support system

Foundations of Psychological Wellness and Resiliency

So how do we develop a psychological model for winning in life? Over the years I've established five foundations of psychological wellness that are often the root cause of issues that eventually appear later in life.

When an overachiever fails—perhaps they get arrested for domestic violence, develop a dangerous addiction, or worse—we often look at the symptom, not the root cause. But the issue has likely originated from one of these five buckets or sources.

If you are a parent, coach or mentor involved with developing a young person, athlete or performer, these are the five things you should keep an eye on as the young person is progressing.

Maturity

This refers to one's understanding and life experience. People without much life experience, wisdom, or exposure to certain aspects may struggle with problem solving or street-wise intelligence.

We see this more frequently in young stars who rise to fame rapidly. Or, in all walks of life, when someone lives in one environment and suddenly shifts to another; it can sometimes be disturbing or disruptive. While there are lots of examples in the celebrity scene, it's relative even on local levels.

Lifestyle

As we've seen, environment and lifestyle are critical to one's wellness and basic health. Psychophysiology—how the body and mind influence each other—impacts our mental wellbeing and the foundation for all we do. Food, health and one's community, environment or living situation can all have an effect. Are your lifestyle habits healthy? Are you getting enough sleep? Are you eating poorly?

Self-esteem

This refers to one's self-worth, insecurities, confidence, and self-respect. Moreover, it is ultimately related to spiritual well-being, identity, and one's sense of self. What is your worldview and understanding of other people? What is your background and upbringing? These perspectives are often most influenced by childhood memories and experiences. Bullying, separations, and more sinister experiences all can have severe and deep-rooted impacts.

Security

One of the most fundamental drivers of behavior is how we perceive security. For many, social standing and financial security are the greatest threats to security. Do you feel secure in your role or position? Do you feel threatened? Self-esteem and security are very closely related. In most cases, security is a matter of perspective—what appears insignificant to one is critical or important to another. What someone may view as irrational actions or behaviors can appear as perfectly rational from your point of view, and vice versa.

Attachment

As a species, we are not designed to survive alone. Some will argue our singular role in life is to extend our species. As a base fundamental driver, we all need support and love to flourish. No one survives or achieves anything alone. Attachment is spirituality, emotional support, love and friendships—all of the personal relationships outside of work and the social network that one relies on.

Back to Control

No one is perfect and no one comes through life unscathed. Everyone has something they have to manage. I've used these five foundations to help identify and assess the deep-seated challenges people face in managing life's obstacles. It is certainly easier to help someone else identify these simply because others can be more objective and help guide others through exploring them.

KNOW WHAT YOU MUST ACCEPT. KNOW WHAT YOU CAN CHANGE

HOLISTIC HIGH ACHIEVER WELLNESS MODEL

Holistic High Achiever Wellness Model

Whether you're working on your own personal challenges or helping someone else, it's important to distinguish whether these issues are either controllable or uncontrollable.

Cases of uncontrollable issues can be those who have a hereditary predisposition (to something such as addiction) or an issue they cannot change. In these cases, we need to find acceptance or help others with acceptance strategies, such as Alcoholics Anonymous meetings, therapy, or other resources that can help one cope.

More often than not, issues that are lifestyle related are controllable, or more controllable than they first appear to be and able to be fixed rather easily. In these situations, we need to implement a change strategy to help fix the lifestyle issue. You can remove or relocate; update or revamp an environment; or alter something like nutrition or other daily habits.

It may be easy to recognize these issues in others, but the hardest part is seeing the signs when they come into your own life. High achievers are their own worst enemy. They do not spot these things. It's one of the biggest challenges that high achievers face, and I've realized this through working with these types of people, and even in reflecting on my own life.

In general, these people have achieved so much by overcoming these issues through brute force. That's what you pride yourself on.

You think, *I can get through this. I'll just work harder and this will go away. This is just a phase I'm going through right now. I'll just avoid this person or thing and go about my business.*

As you'd expect, elite performers and high achievers are very, very good at suppressing any weaknesses that they may have. Whether it's attachment issues, maturity issues, or lifestyle issues, we overcome them. While helping others through problems, we suppress and hide these things and fail to see them in ourselves.

This is very common in elite sports and in the Special Forces community. Because so much of their job and work is predicated on avoiding these issues, they struggle to self-reflect. Suppressing and hiding can work very well for a period of time. But eventually, it will falter and break, leaving you in worse condition than if you recognized—and sought help for—the issue at the beginning.

THE
MIND
AND
BODY
ARE ONE

No One Gets Out Alone

As high achievers, it is difficult for you to identify these shortcomings but it's imperative to identify the signs and also rely on someone else for support. It's one thing to read this and understand it, but it's another to acknowledge that you need a partner to get through. We all need the support of the tribe.

No one gets through life on his or her own without help from others. Not even Navy SEALs.

In May 2014, Naval Admiral William H. McRaven, ninth commander of U.S. Special Operations Command and the one who oversaw the operation that killed Osama bin Laden, gave the commencement speech at The University of Texas at Austin. In speaking to the crowd of students, Adm. McRaven shared a story that explains why you need a good partner or support system to get through life:

"During SEAL training the students are broken down into boat crews. Each crew is seven students—three on each side of a small rubber boat and one coxswain to help guide the dingy.

Every day your boat crew forms up on the beach and is instructed to get through the surf zone and paddle several miles down the coast.

In the winter, the surf off San Diego can get to be 8 to 10 feet high and it is exceedingly difficult to paddle through the plunging surf unless everyone digs in. Every paddle must be synchronized to the stroke count of the coxswain. Everyone must exert equal effort, or the boat will turn against the wave and be unceremoniously tossed back on the beach.

For the boat to make it to its destination, everyone must paddle. You can't change the world alone—you will need some help—and to truly get from your starting point to your destination takes friends, colleagues, the good will of strangers and a strong coxswain to guide them.

If you want to change the world, find someone to help you paddle."

The role of the partner, a fellow sheepdog —the person that will help you paddle—is to be a sensor for you. Because we tend not to see these signs, the role of the other person is to notice and help you recognize the indications that something is wrong or out of sorts. We tend to try to push these people away because we want to overcome things on our own, but we all need to rely on someone who can tell you the truth when you need to hear it.

If you are self-aware, you may notice certain things about yourself during your day-to-day activities. You may notice that your apartment is untidy or a room in your house is accumulating a mess. If you're well attuned with yourself, you'll probably realize when you are more irritable with other people or more easily agitated than normal. Or you'll notice that you are starting to forget things or making simple mental errors at work.

All of these things fall into one of the three areas—spiritual, cognitive, and emotional—that are coming under pressure. These are all signs that one, two or all of these three batteries in your brain are being drained or losing power.

If you are self-aware, you can notice this as it is happening, but most helpful of all is having another person to help point these out to you, because people who are very driven tend to ignore them or overlook them.

YOU ONLY GET ONE SHOT AT LIFE. THIS IS NEITHER A DRILL OR A DRESS REHEARSAL

The Batteries of the Brain

The spiritual, cognitive, and emotional batteries are all developed with different capacities in different people. This distinction is clearly evidenced in so many everyday interactions and situations.

Take, for example, someone who is exceptionally patient or seems to be able to tolerate a lot of emotional stress without any physical or outward evidence. This type of person likely has a huge emotional battery, but even they can still become fatigued. Or, in the case of someone who is able to take on, work through and balance several projects that involve complicated numbers, formulas or information, the cognitive battery is likely at a high capacity.

How do we recognize and notice these things in our daily lives? Reflect on your day.

Perhaps you are coming home from work and you feel unhappy and irritable. If you start to notice yourself feeling easily irritated by minute things that your colleagues do, it is a signal that there are issues on a spiritual level, that values are not aligned with you and the organization.

If you snap at the barista at Starbucks who is not making your coffee quick enough, or you easily lose your cool after the supermarket clerk gives you the wrong change, these are signs that you are likely under quite a bit of emotional stress. If you're starting to make practical errors or misinterpreting information, it is an indication that your cognitive battery is fatigued because of the mental stress you are under.

You can also have spiritual stress or emotional stress that presents itself as cognitive stress. In other words, all of your batteries are starting to fatigue.

But the most important thing in all of this is to listen to a partner, or sensor, that can identify these stresses, or to self-reflect and recognize these things when they happen.

You think, *Okay, I've made a huge numerical error on an invoice I sent out. Why am I making this mistake? Where am I being overloaded right now?*

We use this model to see where we are in terms of our maturity and what areas need most work. So how do we fix it?

If the stress is emotional, we need to switch off and do something that will help us relax. Go watch a movie, read a book, take a bath. Do something to take away any stress and recharge that battery.

If it's cognitive, we need to hand off some work to other people and use our time at work to do things that are not mentally stressful. Listen to something instead of reading; ask a coworker to summarize a lengthy document.

If the stress is spiritual, where someone feels disenfranchised from their social groups, we need to be more open and spend time relating to those in our circle.

Do not isolate. Recharge the spiritual battery by taking time to relate and connect with others. We treat the issue with a solution that is relative to that problem.

Ideas for Action

- *Do I support my mind with healthy food and exercise?*

- *Do I sacrifice sleep and rest for personal achievement?*

- *How different is my public image from my real identity?*

- *Do I feel pressure to project and protect an image?*

- *How do I respond to emotional stress? When do I not do it best? Why?*

- *Do I have a healthy understanding of the 5 foundations?*

- *Do I have the opportunity to develop some of the 5 foundations?*

- *What areas of my life do I need to adopt acceptance strategies?*

- *In which areas should I implement change strategies?*

- *Do I recharge my mental batteries? Or let them run flat?*

Part IV

STORMS & SHEEPDOGS

"And once the storm is over, you won't remember how you made it through, how you managed to survive. You won't even be sure, whether the storm is really over.

But one thing is certain. When you come out of the storm, you won't be the same person who walked in.

That's what this storm's all about."

Haruki Murakami

Riding the Storm

I've already described life as a boat journey through vast oceans. As the captain of your own ship, it's your task to navigate through the seas. You are surrounded by family, friends and loved ones in boats alongside you—the people who care for you, and you for them.

At the helm, the turn of the wheel steers the boat, but you only control this by your reactions to what happens—reactions that influence your decisions, relationships, reactions, and attitudes.

You do not control the sea. You do not control the winds, tides, waves or the weather. These are the uncontrollables on your journey. All you can control is how you react to these elements—that is what turns the wheel. In quiet or stormy seas, that is all you control.

The waters are never completely calm. Storms come unexpectedly and disrupt you and your boat on your journey.

Abrupt, unpredictable, tumultuous, and intense, storms take many shapes and forms.

Perhaps it's a simple rainstorm (a broken appliance in your home; a fender-bender on the road) or maybe it's a more powerful squall, with strong winds, thunder and lightning (a health diagnosis; a sudden job loss). No matter its strength or intensity, storms will come.

The most important thing to remember is that no journey—or no person in life—will carry on without encountering storms of some nature. As the classic song goes: *"Into each life some rain must fall."*

Even when the weather is fair, even in the calm moments after the storm, you must know that at some point, there will always be another storm.

"Damaged people are dangerous. They know they can survive."

Josephine Hart

But what do we do when the storm comes sweeping in without warning? When we are deluged by the magnitude of what occurred? When the storm is so devastating and destructive that we are crippled? When life comes at you fast and you are struck by a traumatic event or occurrence, you must take a moment to refer back to the five foundations of psychological wellness—maturity, lifestyle, self-esteem, security and attachment—and remember that you'll need support from those closest to your boat for advice and help to get through.

AFTER THE STORM, THERE WILL BE ANOTHER STORM

While traumatic experiences can be unforeseen incidents or circumstances—like a car accident causing injuries or fatalities, or an unexpected diagnosis of cancer—a storm can also gain strength and develop up over time due to your own actions, resulting in a more self-inflicted traumatic event in your life.

Let's take Peter as an example. Peter is stressed out from his job and turns to a relatively safe stimulus to provide a surge of pleasure as a coping mechanism: food. Over the span of 18 months, he ends up putting on 35 pounds. Then, at a routine doctor's visit, an alarming health issue is discovered due to the unhealthy weight gain. The traumatic event is clearly the concerning diagnosis, but it's also clear that the storm was building and building for quite some time, due to stresses stemming from Peter's reaction to his workplace.

The Perseverance Paradox

Life will always bring storms, no matter what. But sheepdogs who are elite performers or high achievers are liable to more risk than most. They push hard for periods of time and manage stress to achieve targets and goals. But operating at high levels of pressure exposes them to greater risk when unforeseen storms come. Under extreme pressure, we rely on our foundations of wellness and any limitations can be exposed.

The challenge many high achievers have is that they have trained or been trained to push through discomfort and suppress any issues that may arise. We all know there are times to persevere. Under pressure, the body reacts and relies on its primal 'fight or flight' instinct. No one achieves anything without enduring difficulty or hardship. However there is a difference between short-term perseverance and prolonged stress without respite.

Hans Selye, a medical doctor and researcher, developed a theory of General Adaptation Syndrome (GAS). He proposed that there were three stages: alarm reaction, resistance, and exhaustion.

The alarm reaction stage refers to the initial symptoms the body produces when under stress—that's the 'fight or flight' response. In the resistance stage, your body begins to recover from the stress but remains on high alert. The exhaustion stage is the final result of prolonged stress over long periods—signs of this include fatigue, anxiety, and depression.

High performers naturally push through the second stage of general adaptation syndrome and don't actually resolve the stressful situation at hand. They just deal with it. Many become good at tolerating this for a long period of time through training and motivation.

But even though it may seem like the situation is being dealt with, the body is actually remaining on high alert and over an extended period of time, it can become used to living with high stress levels. This is not good. You may think you are managing the stress well, but without actually resolving the issue, your body will eventually reach a point where it cannot tolerate any more pressure.

Over time, constant exposure to stress leads to either an internal biological response, such as physical illness, or a behavioral emotional response. This is the breaking point. Generally, the nature of the exhaustion is related to the intensity of the stress.

What Seyle Didn't Say

Interestingly, there's an ironic paradox to this model when it comes to elite performers, one Selye didn't identify: when the stressor is suddenly removed or resolved, there can be a negative reaction.

You'll see this often with members of elite military units returning to civilian life after deployment. When the stress or pressure is suddenly removed—i.e., the soldier is sent home from the demanding, rigorous, and high-alert military lifestyle—the person finds this abrupt change unsettling.

The reaction can be emotional, behavioral, or physical. For people who are trained to tolerate discomfort, this can be perceived physiologically as another challenge to overcome, but it can sometimes be too taxing to manage safely. In other cases, in order to counter the disconcerting feeling, some people seek other activities or engage in risky behavior.

Let's take a step back for a moment. We've learned about the five foundations of psychological wellness, how they are typically the root cause of an issue in life and how to use this model for helping others work through their issues.

As in Peter's example, the root cause—the actual, legitimate source of the problem—can actually lead to a traumatic or major life incident. But that root cause typically goes through a series of steps before it leads to something serious or substantial in your life. We can examine this series of steps and follow the pathway back to the five foundations of psychological wellness, which will ultimately help us in dealing with any storms we may encounter along the way. Let's take a look.

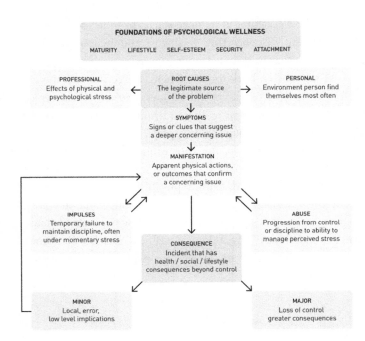

Foundations of Psychological Wellness

Left of Boom

If we follow this model and work backwards, it's easy to see the progression. Let's start with Consequence—the end result or ramification that could potentially take form as a major incident.

In Peter's case, the consequence was the doctor's unfortunate discovery of a serious health issue in his body. Perhaps it is a legal issue, where someone commits a crime or offense and is arrested for his or her actions. Maybe a relationship ended in divorce or there was a fire that overtook an entire building.

What's important to recognize about this is that there are two types of consequences: one that we are aware of and we admit to when it becomes apparent; and one that we are not aware of or willing to accept. For example, someone may have an addiction that they don't want to admit to, or a failing marriage that is effectively over. In other words, ignoring an issue or not admitting to it does not make it go away. It is still a consequence.

In some cases it's because of impulse control, where in a moment of rashness or state of extreme pressure, someone reacts destructively and there are immediate negative consequences. In high performers, however, there is often a pattern leading up to the actual event.

Before the consequence occurred however, there was an Abuse. An abuse is a progression from management of an issue to the negative impact of the issue. Maybe it's an abuse of unhealthy foods; it could also be relationships, alcohol, or drugs. Perhaps someone in a pressure-filled situation acted in an adverse way through violent, self-destructive or harmful actions. Abuse is repeated negative actions.

Taking a step backwards from the point of abuse is the stage of Manifestation, or the phase when there is a physical sign or indication of an issue that is now apparent or visible to others. This is where relationships are critical.

If you surround yourself with good people who you trust, they should be able to notice when something is wrong or unusual with you. Our friends and loved ones often see these clues before others who are not as familiar with us do.

Perhaps a friend notices that you look more tired recently, like you haven't been getting enough sleep. Or your significant other sees you turning to a bottle of wine after work to relieve stress, instead of your usual gym session. Those around us should be able to see we are under pressure and start to see cracks in our normal demeanor.

ALWAYS GO TO THE SOURCE. FIND THE WHY

Before the manifestation phase is the Symptoms stage, where there are signs and clues that arise that we may notice about ourselves. This is the point of self-awareness where you feel like there may be an issue that is affecting you or the people around you. These are small signs that you are under a lot of psychological pressure or stress—those around you won't notice them quite yet.

Maybe you can't sleep and you spend time tossing and turning instead of resting through the night. Perhaps you find yourself reaching for an extra cup of coffee or you are more irritable with others. It could be something that you're forgetting to do, like adding detergent to your load of laundry.

For me, I know I am starting to overburden myself when my apartment is untidy. This is a very simply identifiable everyday signal I notice. Of course, in practice it means that I am simply rushing too much and wasn't taking the time to take care of basic tasks.

A special operations guy I worked with used to tell me that he would know he was clearly demonstrating symptoms when he would come home and notice his dogs weren't friendly or as responsive as they normally were to him. His pets noticed and sensed that he was irritable, ill-tempered, and unhappy. Those of us who are self-aware may notice these signs first. But many of us ignore or push them away or become so preoccupied we never see them. When others start to notice, that's when the manifestation occurs.

Now we get to the key issue—we want to move 'left of boom.' We want to get to the source, the cause of the issue. Eventually, these stages lead us back to the Root Cause, which we've determined to be the actual, legitimate source of the problem.

One of these five things is causing this issue that is presenting itself, first as a symptom to you, then as a manifestation, which then becomes an abuse, where you start to reach for something. Then that abuse can result in a major incident or serious consequence.

Treat the Source, Not the Symptom

When something happens, we automatically focus on the event and draw conclusions from it. However, the action often hides underlying, more deeply-rooted issues. For instance, the abuse of narcotics or alcohol is the symptom, not the cause of the issue. In order to help address and manage root causes, we can't just treat the issue or activity—in this example, the substance abuse problem— we have to dive deeper into the root cause.

The root cause usually extends from one of five areas: a maturity, lifestyle, self-esteem, security, or attachment issue. Generally, one or more of these five causes is the root of the issue presenting itself—first as a symptom to you, then as a manifestation which others may see, which develops into abuse.

Eventually, if left untreated, the abuse will lead to a loss of control, where the person continues to knowingly partake in behaviors that can lead to destructive consequences. These can be consequences that are covered up or simply go unnoticed to others, which can lead to a major incident or serious consequence.

The consequence can happen in one of two ways: sometimes it is a constant or repeating event, while other times it's a one-off or impulse that happens once, before change strategies are implemented.

Take Tiger Woods for example. Before November, 2009, Woods was the epitome of a successful star athlete: he was setting records and racking up championships on the course; he had one of the largest endorsement contracts ever, at that time; he was well liked by peers, fans and the media. But one night in '09, everything came crashing down. But as we later found out, this major consequence was after a series of minor consequences.

That Thanksgiving night, Woods' then-wife, Elin Nordegren, suspected he was cheating with a NYC nightclub manager named Rachel Uchitel. As the story goes, Woods took an Ambien and fell asleep and Nordegren took his phone and scrolled for Uchitel's number. She messaged with her and then called, catching her husband in a lie and confirming his extramarital affair.

Woods woke up and he and Nordegren began arguing and physically fighting, until Woods ran out of the house and got into his brand new Escalade. He sped out of the driveway, crashed into the curb and then a fire hydrant, before hitting a tree.

After Nordegren pulled Woods out of the car, bloody and unconscious, Woods was ticketed for careless driving. In the days that followed, more claims of Woods' multiple affairs surfaced. From there, Woods' career began its downward spiral. Woods had reached the final stage—a major incident with serious implications.

"I stopped living according to my core values. I knew what I was doing was wrong but thought only about myself and thought I could get away with whatever I wanted to."

Tiger Woods

As we've seen, the widely-reported addiction to promiscuity and relationship abuse was not the root cause. In many cases, we are left with one or a combination of the five core issues: maturity, lifestyle, self-esteem, security, or attachment. As we've learned, these are largely controllable and can be manageable with the right help.

HOLISTIC HIGH ACHIEVER WELLNESS MODEL

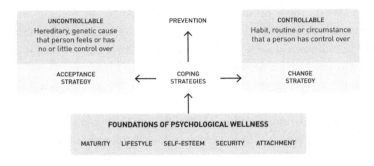

Holistic High Achiever Wellness Model

As with many celebrities and public-facing figures, we often don't hear about situations like this until the major incident occurs —if we ever do at all. Most people of this stature have the means to cover up and hide manifestations along the way. But when the major event takes place, it is sometimes revealed that there were clues that something was just waiting to happen.

In Woods' case, perhaps those close to him saw and knew there were signs along the way. But so goes the paradox with high achievers: they can appear intimidating, so few have the moral courage to speak truth to power.

SOMETIMES, EVEN A SHEEPDOG NEEDS A SHEEPDOG

How to Help

It is our duty to look out for those in our own circle and ask questions when we suspect problems—not in a pointed way, but in a supportive way. Questioning style is important with high achievers. Many want to get help or realize they are losing composure, but they don't want to admit it and feel as though they are letting go of control.

Saying, "You seem to be more stressed. How can I help?" can appear like you are challenging their authority. A more relaxed approach is better; allowing the conversation to develop naturally usually leads to an environment where the high performer will feel more comfortable. When we are experiencing these issues, this is where our fellow trusted sheepdogs can help us.

Now that we understand the pathway and how the five foundations of psychological wellness are directly related to traumatic events, it's time to face the storm.

The Sheepdog and The Storm

Throughout my career I have learned many valuable lessons in high performance from some of the best athletes, coaches, operators, and businessmen in the world.

As I began to realize success was based on the holistic attributes, not simply excellence in one area alone, it also became apparent that wellness of the whole person was the most important foundation for a sustainable, long-lasting and successful career.

Whether it's in sport, military, or business, the world's best can perform the chosen professional tasks exceptionally well. They rarely fail in completing the task at hand and they have the ability to execute under pressure.

But during the times they did fail 'in the field,' I started to notice that the actual root cause wasn't actually a performance issue, it was a wellness issue. Having developed a deep understanding of performance at every level, the goal was now to help build a resiliency lifestyle model for the high performers and organizations I was coaching.

Ironically, understanding this taught me the most important lesson for high achievers: we are the worst at helping ourselves avoid these challenges. I was a coach the best called on to help them perform, avoid fatigue and burnout, and yet I had no coach myself.

"When I see people stand fully in their truth, or when I see someone fall down, get back up, and say, 'Damn. That really hurt, but this is important to me and I'm going in again'—my gut reaction is, 'What a badass.'"

Brene Brown

In 2018, I didn't see myself falling into the trap I was helping others avoid. I was so focused on others and my work I wasn't either looking after myself, nor had I my own sheepdogs looking out for me.

At the time, I was working in two positions for the University of Michigan football program: director of performance, managing the strength and conditioning, sports science, nutrition, and player welfare for the team; and director of operations, overseeing the organization of team functions, events, meal planning, travel and more. Both are dedicated, separate roles in themselves. Trying to do more than I should have, I took on both.

Each job could take up a full-time work week alone, but combining them together, I was working 14-to-16-hour days, seven days a week, year-round. My girlfriend, who also worked at the University, was going through a difficult time in her own life. I did my best to cheer her up, distracting her from her troubles as I juggled the workload of both jobs.

It's safe to say: both personally and professionally, I was under pressure—more than I was aware of. Or, perhaps more accurately, more than I wanted to admit.

But this wasn't anything unusual, I'd always been a high achiever. I was always able to do more than others. In retrospect, I was being drained spiritually, emotionally, and cognitively and I wasn't taking time to refuel these three batteries.

REFUSE TO BE A VICTIM

I relied on the one ability I had always had: the ability to tolerate extreme stress. I had been working in the high-performance sector for such a long time. I was used to being under pressure. I could handle it. In fact, I thrived on it.

I enjoyed being able to solve the most difficult problems, provide solutions and serve as a support system to help others achieve their goals—especially when the pressure was greatest. As we have seen, when your purpose is clear, eustress—which literally means 'good stress'—is manageable and even beneficial.

"Man is many things, but he is not rational."

Oscar Wilde

We know about the importance of values and how being surrounded by people who do not share the same values can result in your spiritual battery constantly being drained. For me, the storm came out of nowhere. Without warning, someone brought to my attention that one of my positions, director of operations, was advertised online.

With one of my jobs apparently no longer mine, I was confused about my job security. Cognitively, trying to manage both a performance and an operations department was a demanding mental task each day. Taking all of those things into consideration, you can, I can now retrospectively, clearly see that my three psychological batteries were fatigued.

Because of the long hours and requirements of the two jobs, my lifestyle was already at its limit—I was running on four to six hours of sleep a night—so the capacity for added resilience wasn't there.

After I found my job advertised online, I went to see the head coach and athletic director to try and get an answer. With the support of donors and regents, I presented the athletic director with a proposal and he said he'd get back to me.

But 40 minutes after I left his office, I got a text from his assistant asking if I could move out of my office to open up space for a new hire. He said I would relocate to a new office after I returned from a speaking engagement in Tampa, Florida, the following week.

No Man's Land

I returned from the event and waited at home for word from the athletic director or his assistants, but nothing came. One week turned into two. The typical daily stress of work, being around friends and constant energy and excitement from players and coaches—which I had thrived on previously—were now removed, and a new stress of uncertainty and unknown had replaced it.

YOU WILL EITHER WIN OR LEARN. BOTH ARE OPPORTUNITY

This was completely new territory for me. No focus. No work to fill my day. Why didn't I tell anyone about my troubles? Honestly, I was just being a lone sheepdog. I didn't lean on the people closest to me because I did not want to add any more worry or pressure to their stresses. I didn't call my parents or family in Ireland and voice my worries to them either, I didn't want to burden or worry them, especially since they were thousands of miles away.

This is what we do, right? We protect those we care about. I thought, *I'm going to get through this. Just like I always have.*

By the third week I was having trouble falling asleep. I went from being around people and friends constantly at work to being all alone for long days. Without the challenges of work that would normally occupy my mind, I'd wake up frequently at night and start thinking trying to understand what was going to happen. The stress and pressures were bubbling up.

Eventually, one morning, after three completely sleepless nights, I turned to alcohol, hoping it would turn off my thoughts and help me sleep. The next morning, I realized I was in trouble. I was losing control of the situation and not thinking clearly.

I finally decided to open up fully to my girlfriend and explain how badly this was now affecting me after four weeks of isolation and uncertainty. I drove the three blocks to her house to finally ask for her help. But I had drank far too much and waited too long.

As I got in the car, I crashed just a block from her house and was arrested. My life was just about to turn upside down.

"The friend in my adversity I shall always cherish most. I can better trust those who helped to relieve the gloom of my dark hours than those who are so ready to enjoy with me the sunshine of my prosperity."

Ulysses S. Grant

I had made a huge mistake. I was fortunate that in my stupidity and recklessness didn't injure anyone. Now I had to face the legal and media fallout, the professional repercussions and the personal embarrassment. Of course, no one knew what I had tried to battle with for the previous four weeks. I was used to pushing to the limit and solving problems on my own.

Little did I know that even though the forced social isolation for four weeks before my recklessness was tough, I was just about to face much longer period—over 12 months—of even greater isolation.

Shortly after the media storm and some initial support, my relationship ended, too. I was utterly alone. Few things are as truly lonely as spending Thanksgiving, Christmas, and New Years by yourself miles from family.

I had no one to blame but myself, however. I made a mistake. Now I had to pay the price. This was the most difficult period of my life.

It's said, 'adversity reveals character.' I can attest to that, and not just your own character, but those around you. As William McRaven said, "We all need teammates to help us."

I was lucky enough to have people whom I had worked with—special forces operators, NFL players and NBA coaches—come forward to help talk me through what I was dealing with.

Almost every single person who contacted me shared their vulnerabilities and stories of mistakes or challenges they'd overcome. This helped me understand a very important lesson: we all encounter storms on our journey through life.

"When one door of happiness closes, another opens, but often we look so long at the closed door that we do not see the one that has been opened for us."

Helen Keller

A few months later I found myself in the middle of a small room surrounded by a group of the world's most experienced special forces operators. I had been working with them on stress and performance under pressure. At the end, one of the guys made a request that caught me by surprise.

"Fergus, tell the guys what happened to you a few months back."

My heart skipped a beat.

Then I told them the whole story.

When I finished I looked around the room. The most senior officer, 45 years old, a veteran of 18 years of war, looked me straight in the eye.

"That is exactly what happens to us, too."

He continued, "Often many of us, rather than lean on others when we need to most, try to do it all alone."

High achievers often are the last to look for support.

RUN OR HIDE FROM YOUR CHOICES AND YOU ARE DESTINED TO REPEAT THEM

Doctor Heal Thyself

In the weeks and months that followed I had a choice, face my mistakes and learn from them or run and make excuses. I knew what the right thing to do was.

The first step was facing the reality of the situation—I could not go back and change what I had done. I could not play the victim either. I had plenty of chances to reach out to others. I reflected on my identity and my purpose. Many people have their identity tied up in their profession alone; they identify as a soldier, or as an accountant. But that is not who a person is—it is what they do.

There were certainly some truly tough and dark days during those months. The first thing that comes naturally to me is automatically searching for positives in any situation. In this case, I was given the opportunity to go in a different direction in my career and help others.

Coincidently, this was something I always intended to do. In fact, it was the purpose of the new role I'd proposed to the athletic director. I wanted to help protect the welfare of all student athletes. But now I had the chance to bring that mission to a wider audience and impact many more people. I started to view the whole event as a blessing. Everything I had lost gave me the opportunity to move in a new direction.

I also learned an important lesson: while I was resilient, I had a limit. I admitted that I needed support and I turned to the true sheepdogs around me. I used my emotions and energy to move forward, and as I did, I kept my focus on my reaffirmed purpose and what was truly important.

Many people look at this story and see it as a tragic negative event. It was a reckless and stupid act. It was also a blessing for me. It presented me with an opportunity for a lesson—if I chose to view it in that way, of course.

I was now surrounded by genuine people who were there for me when I needed them and there for me for who I was. Men and women who I'd helped reached out and in many cases reminded me of the lessons I'd taught them at similar times, something I'll be forever grateful for.

"The most beautiful people we have known are those who have known defeat, known suffering, known struggle, known loss, and have found their way out of the depths.

These persons have an appreciation, a sensitivity, and an understanding of life that fills them with compassions, gentleness, and a deep loving concern.

Beautiful people do not just happen."

Elizabeth Kubler-Ross

The Cobbler's Children

It's an interesting dynamic, isn't it? I was the one who was supposed to be the expert in this area, and even I couldn't spot these shortcomings and signs in myself. That's why it is essential for you to realize that you cannot do it alone.

When the storms come, everyone needs help getting through. You can't sacrifice your own welfare taking care of loved ones. Relationships need to be equal, complimentary. Work can't be a constant drain on you; your values must align.

"What is a friend? A single soul dwelling in two bodies."

Aristotle

I don't share my story with you for praise or sympathy. Quite frankly, it's the opposite. It's my greatest embarrassment. I'm sharing it to show that sometimes, when we think we have it all figured out, we fail to recognize these issues within ourselves.

There's an old saying: "The cobbler's children have the worst shoes." In other words, those of us who should know best sometimes can't help ourselves. As I said in my 2019 TED Talk about the events and my experience: "Sometimes, even sheepdogs need a sheepdog."

Navigating the Storm

When any type of unforeseen event occurs, whether it is initiated by our actions or not, we are faced with choices. As Epictetus, Stockdale, and others have shown us, we have very little control over the world, but we have complete control over how we view things that happen.

When any type of unforeseen event occurs, you can turn to the following steps to overcome it, no matter the shape or severity of the storm. I've used this model to help others get over traumatic events and to cope with the consequences of my own actions.

"Start by doing what's necessary; then do what's possible; and suddenly you are doing the impossible."

Francis of Assisi

Don't be a victim. Learn

Take responsibility. The single biggest mistake people make is failing to accept reality. The most important thing you need to do is accept what you did or accept the situation that happened.

What makes this so difficult is the emotional charge that is associated with it. You can't change the situation, but you can control how you react. Don't blame the storm. There's no point in standing up in the boat and shouting out to the seas about the winds and the rain. Instead, take ownership of the situation.

That's my mistake. I shouldn't have done it and I've no excuse. Or, *It sucks that this happened, but I can't change it. So how can I respond in a positive and productive way?*

You must accept the situation and begin to move forward. You can't sit and wait for the storm to pass and bleed out. It's going to be tough, but you can't make excuses or blame others for your mistakes or for what has occurred. If you choose to be a victim for even a split second, you'll never get through it.

RESILIENCE IS FAILING FAST AND FURIOUS, THEN FAILING DIFFERENTLY THE NEXT TIME

Be Strong

Once you accept that you are not a victim, you have to be strong and stay focused. Stand up and face the situation as it is, not as you might want it to be. Don't back down. Lean on your identity and purpose and figure out your goal.

I like to say: there is no such thing as defense, only offense when you don't have the ball. Accept the consequences of your actions or the fallout from the event and pay the price.

You will be filled with all kinds of emotions: confusion, shame, sadness, despair, anger, and disillusionment. Work your way through these and then take emotion out of the equation. Look at things factually. Then continue picking up the pieces.

Be aware that things may get worse. After the storm, there's always going to be another storm. Stay strong. You are now armed with the knowledge that you are fallible and vulnerable.

Knowing who you are and what you are here to do in life will keep you strong during the tough times. Because when everything else is taken away from you, your purpose are what drives you to keep going forward.

"Vulnerability is not winning or losing; it's having the courage to show up and be seen when we have no control over the outcome."

Brene Brown

Survive

When the storm is bad, sometimes all you have to do is simply survive. There will be times when everything is extremely overwhelming or stressful. There will be moments when you feel alone, when it seems as though there is little hope. You may lose a loved one or receive terrible medical news.

On those days, just concentrate on surviving. Keep your identity and purpose at the forefront of your mind. As an operator once told me, "Even if you're down on your knees, never roll onto your back." Never give up. You just have to survive and regroup.

"We tend to forget that happiness doesn't come as a result of getting something we don't have, but rather of recognizing and appreciating what we do have."

Frederick Keonig

Find the Good

No matter the trauma, there's always a positive. If you lose someone close to you, you can reflect on the good memories you shared when you were together. You can look around at how they brought people together for you. You need to learn from the experience and be honest with yourself and identify your mistakes.

In my case, I realized too late that I wasn't keeping any kind of balance in life, and, in doing so, I sacrificed my relationships and my health.

You will pay a price for such hard-won lessons, but the value you can take from them can be of immeasurable value—if you choose to frame it that way. There are a lot of positives that come from any traumatic event and you need to find them in your circumstances.

"Never be bullied into silence. Never allow yourself to be made a victim. Accept no one's definition of your life but define yourself."

Harvey Fierstein

AUTHENTIC PEOPLE AREN'T PERFECT. PERFECT PEOPLE AREN'T AUTHENTIC

You will need support

For many, this will be one of the hardest things to accept during this process. It involves admitting vulnerability, and accepting the outstretched hand when it is there.

The people who are going to stay in the boat and help you navigate the storm, the ones who will still be there when the storm passes, those are the sheepdogs you must turn to in times of need. Sheep will scatter and wolves will circle, as they will try to exploit the difficult times that you are in. But the people who stay to help are the true sheepdogs you can trust—and you're going to need them, whether you like to admit it or not.

For most high achievers, self-reliance is a positive and always dependable trait. But you must accept the reality that you will not get through this without help and support from others. This is why accepting your vulnerability is important.

Don't worry about what others think

Outside of your inner circle, there will be people who whisper and gossip, who try to discredit you or exploit your challenges. Sheepdogs don't worry about the opinions of sheep.

Very often when a traumatic situation occurs, we get distracted and overwhelmed by what others think. We get worried about the opinions of people who don't matter. Keep the focus on what is truly important—your identity and purpose in life—and only worry about the people close to you.

Move on

When the storm passes, sometimes you just have to keep rowing. Or burn the boats. You just have to move forward and move on. This is why your identity and purpose are critical. Knowing who you are and what is important for you gives you a purpose to strive towards and the motivation to have a positive impact. You can't wait for something pivotal to happen. Instead, use your emotion and energy to learn from your mistakes and progress through life as a new and improved version of yourself—one who has weathered the storm and is now equipped to handle whatever comes next.

"One day, two monks set out for a temple in a valley beyond the woods. While cutting a pathway through the woods, they came across a choppy stream they needed to cross. There, stood by the bank of the stream, was a beautiful young maiden dressed in silk. She was clearly at a loss as to how to cross without getting muddy and wet.

So, without thinking twice, the elder monk gestured to pick her up. Shocked, she obliged. He put her over his shoulder and waded across to the other side. The younger monk, dismayed and uneasy at what he had witnessed, followed in tow.

Upon reaching the other side of the bank, the elder monk put the maiden down gently. The maiden paid her respects and walked on. The monks then continued on their way to the temple.

As they navigated through the forest, the younger monk, still troubled by what he'd seen, asked, 'How could you do that? We aren't even supposed to make eye contact with women, let alone pick them up and carry them!'

Without a thought, the elder monk turned to the younger monk and said, 'Oh, are you still carrying her? I put her down when I reached the other side of the stream.'

And with that, the elder monk turned and continued leading the way through the forest, leaving the younger monk to contemplate his words for the remainder of the journey."

The Oxygen Mask

When you're sitting on an airplane waiting to take off, it's likely that you'll hear the standard in-flight safety protocols from a flight attendant or video on the TV screen.

We've all heard them so many times that it's easy to ignore, but the instructions clearly state: "Put on your own oxygen mask first, before helping others." This is because your job, first and foremost, is to take care of yourself. Unless you are healthy and stable, you cannot take care of anyone else.

Ideas for Action

- *Do I allow myself to become fatigued or am I truly healthy?*

- *Am I addressing the source of the challenges or the symptoms?*

- *What are my blind spots?*

- *Who are the sheepdogs that can help me identify them?*

- *Am I better at giving advice than receiving it?*

- *Am I a victim? Or do I take responsibility?*

- *Am I truly accepting and comfortable being wrong?*

- *Do I look for the good in all people and situations?*

Part V

THE SUCCESS EQUATION

"True happiness is to enjoy the present, without anxious dependence upon the future, not to amuse ourselves with either hopes or fears but to rest satisfied with what we have, which is sufficient, for he that is so wants nothing.

The greatest blessings of mankind are within us and within our reach.

A wise man is content with his lot, whatever it may be, without wishing for what he has not."

Seneca

True Happiness

Happiness truly lies at the center of our world—even though we may lose sight of it from time to time. As Aristotle famously said, "Happiness is the meaning and the purpose of life, the whole aim and end of human existence."

If asked to explain the purpose of life, few people would readily say happiness—most would consider wealth or recognition first and foremost.

What do we really mean by happiness? My good friend Brett Steenbarger, the associate professor of psychiatry and behavioral sciences at SUNY Upstate Medical University in Syracuse, New York, explains it further: "In this context, the opposite of happiness is not sadness, but rather a certain kind of emotional dis-ease—a vague but pervasive existential guilt that you're letting life's opportunities slip by, that you're settling for less than you rightfully should."

It may seem counterintuitive to explore happiness with a discussion about death. But as Australian palliative care nurse Bronnie Ware learned during the many years she spent with patients during the last three to twelve weeks of their lives, mortality can be incredibly insightful and thought-provoking.

As she chronicled in a blog post that eventually turned into a 2012 book, *The Top Five Regrets of the Dying: A Life Transformed by the Dearly Departing*, Ware's life was transformed by the people she was caring for. No longer receiving medical care and sent home to die, Ware's patients experienced a range of emotions, but each one ultimately found their peace before departing.

What were the lessons of those who had lived? What were the thoughts or regrets of those facing death? In her time with each patient, Ware would ask questions about any regrets they had or what they would do differently if they could go back and do it all over again.

Not surprisingly, she found some shared themes that repeatedly emerged from her conversations. It is from these most common five regrets that we can learn how to strive for—and ultimately arrive at—true contentment and peace of mind with our lives and ourselves, each and every day.

1. "I wish I'd had the courage to live a life true to myself, not the life others expected of me."

We often remark that we "didn't know someone well." But how well do you truly know yourself? Understanding your identity and who you are is one of the most important aspects of living a fulfilling life. Are you living your life to fulfill your own dreams, or the dreams of society's expectations or someone else?

Ware says that this was the most common regret of all—when people realize that their time is near expiration, they start to reflect on the choices they made and the things they did or did not do as a result. Be true to yourself and have the authenticity to live that life

—not according to what others, social media or somebody else says, but according to who you are as a person at heart.

2. "I wish I hadn't worked so hard."

One realization that Ware discovered was connected to how people used their time and their purpose in life. Are you working to live or living to work?

Ware says that this regret was most common among male patients—particularly those who had missed out on their children's childhood and development, or overlooked a relationship with a partner, all because of over-commitment to a job or career.

Just as you must live life according to who you are, you must also carry out each day according to your true purpose. Of course, income and finances are always a factor in determining the balance between work and life.

But by creating more time and space in your life for connections and more personal commodities, you will become happier and can avoid this regret later in life. To this end, true wealth isn't having disposable income—it's having disposable time.

> "Time you enjoy wasting is not wasted time."
>
> Marthe Troly-Curtin

3. "I wish I'd had the courage to express my feelings."

Ware found many of those in their final weeks regretted not being more open, genuine, and authentic about their feelings. In a world where openness is mistaken for weakness, vulnerability is often difficult for us to embrace. Who wants to be vulnerable? It's uncomfortable. It's risky. It makes us feel uncertain and exposed.

But the reality is, vulnerability is actually a pathway that opens us up to feelings that are just the opposite of those uneasy ones: joy, empathy, and courage. By suppressing feelings or detaching ourselves from others, we actually push away people or foster unhealthy relationships, ultimately leading to isolation and unhappiness.

Instead, it is important to be genuine and face the situations that may make you feel susceptible and weak. You must open yourself up to developing loving relationships in your life. As Dr. Brené Brown, a research professor at the University of Houston and author of five *New York Times* best-sellers, famously said: "What makes you vulnerable makes you beautiful."

"Since you get more joy out of giving joy to others, you should put a good deal of thought into the happiness that you are able to give."

Eleanor Roosevelt

STRIVE NOT FOR HAPPINESS. STRIVE FOR CONTENTMENT

4. "I wish I had stayed in touch with my friends."

During the final weeks of one's life, the list of things that matter grows short. Money, work, status, belongings and possessions easily fall off and become unimportant.

In the end, it is the relationships and the people around you that remain. It is important to remember that as we move along in our fast-paced and hectic lives.

Oftentimes, people with busy lifestyles sacrifice time spent with friends and family. But the love and connections you have with those in your inner circle are some of the most valuable parts of your life—ones that you should be cherishing long before you are faced with death.

5. "I wish that I had let myself be happier."

It's interesting that the final regret of the dying is that many wished they had let themselves be happier. The realization that we are in control of our happiness is quite profound and echoes Aristotle's quote, "Happiness depends upon ourselves."

We control our reaction to life and its events. Are you choosing to be happy, or simply going with the familiar flow of your everyday life and pretending to be content? It is time to take control of your happiness and let go of the things that are holding you back. The most important thing is to love yourself first and be happy first. These are decisions in life, not circumstances.

Over the years, I have come to realize that the greatest trap in our life is not success, popularity, or power, but self-rejection.

Success, popularity, and power can indeed present a great temptation, but their seductive quality often comes from the way they are part of the much larger temptation to self-rejection.

When we have come to believe in the voices that call us worthless and unlovable, then success, popularity, and power are easily perceived as attractive solutions. The real trap, however, is self-rejection.

As soon as someone accuses me or criticizes me, as soon as I am rejected, left alone, or abandoned, I find myself thinking, "Well, that proves once again that I am a nobody." ... [My dark side says,] I am no good... I deserve to be pushed aside, forgotten, rejected, and abandoned.

Self-rejection is the greatest enemy of the spiritual life because it contradicts the sacred voice that calls us the Beloved. Being the Beloved constitutes the core truth of our existence."

Henri J.M. Nouwen

Happiness vs. Pleasure vs. Contentment

Ware's discovery of these five regrets is truly powerful. How can we harness this knowledge and use it to address these issues while we still have the time?

Let's begin with a simple clarification: Happiness is really about finding contentment. Happiness is not an event. It's a life's work; it's the total sum of all we do. Once you accept this, you'll begin to see happiness as a journey, not as a destination.

The first step in finding contentment is realizing that it's not a place you reach and then subsequently stay there forever. It's a mindset. What does this mean? Life is never going to be perfect, smooth and 100% untroubled. There is no red pushpin, no final stop on the road to happiness with a big, shiny gate and bright, beaming sign welcoming you to your destination. There are always going to be challenges in life, just based on its nature and chaos.

James Stockdale said something related to this that paints the picture for us. As a Navy pilot and commander, Stockdale is one of the most decorated military leaders, but it was his time spent as a prisoner of war in North Vietnam that taught him valuable lessons about life's challenges and one's search for contentment. When asked about the people who struggled the most in captivity, Stockdale responded, with little hesitation: the optimists.

As James Collins describes it in his book, *Good to Great,* Stockdale said:

> *They were the ones who said, 'We're going to be out by Christmas.' And Christmas would come, and Christmas would go.*
>
> *Then they'd say, 'We're going to be out by Easter.' And Easter would come, and Easter would go.*
>
> *And then Thanksgiving, and then it would be Christmas again. And they died of a broken heart.*
>
> *This is a fundamental lesson. You must never confuse faith that you will prevail in the end—which you can never afford to lose—with the discipline to confront the most brutal facts of your current reality, whatever they might be.*

This has become known as the Stockdale Paradox. Expect the best but be prepared for the worst.

AUTHENTICITY IS WHEN YOUR PUBLIC IMAGE AND PERSONAL IDENTITY ARE ALIGNED

Flow and Happiness

When you recognize and accept that there will always be unhappy and challenging moments and traumatic events in life, you realize that the main objective is to find contentment, not happiness. To find that feeling of being at peace. It's about finding—and living in—that balanced zone.

Hungarian-American psychologist Mihaly Csikszentmihalyi used a similar idea of "living in the zone" with his concept of *flow*, a highly focused mental state that he says is integral to creating genuine happiness.

Csikszentmihalyi found that when people are at their most creative and most productive—or in this state of flow—they are also often at their happiest, even if they are involved in a challenging task. When people are in chaotic and demanding situations—think of a soldier in a battle or an athlete during a competitive game—the goal is not happiness, it is a content state where the mind is at ease and operating at an optimal level, despite the environment or situation.

"There is only one way to happiness and that is to cease worrying about things which are beyond the power of our will."

Epictetus

Csikszentmihalyi's concept of flow helps emphasize a critical aspect of contentment: constant happiness is an illusion. It's like expecting to win every single game, every single year. It's not going to happen.

Even after a storm, there's always going to be another storm. Even in the midst of my struggles after my own experiences, where I lost everything professionally and personally, I knew that there was going to be a calm day when the sun was going to come out. But I also knew that there was going to be another storm somewhere down the line. Everything isn't going to be perfect, but contentment is about being able to accept that, temper expectations, and live in the moment, without a long list of unreasonable desires.

The other challenge with happiness is the frequent confusion with pleasure. Due to the essence of human nature and the society and culture we live in, happiness and pleasure are often conflated. Think of all of the things in our lives that promise happiness with the press of a button, a simple purchase, a swig or a bite; happy hour; hitting that 'like' button on social media; popping a pill for relief; buying something new; or indulging in an entire pint of Ben and Jerry's ice cream.

All of these things—food, drugs, social media, shopping, and more—may have an immediate, instant effect on your happiness. Sure, the pint of ice cream tastes delicious. Those new shoes you bought make you feel good about yourself. And they were such a good deal! But, in reality, those feelings are all fleeting. That's because they are a result of pleasure-seeking activities.

Pleasure is a good feeling. It is short-lived. It can be experienced alone and can be attained with material items or behaviors. It is visceral. Contentment is achieved through long-term effort, not through the practice of hedonism of the present, or pleasure for the moment. It is an accomplishment and a form of excellence. It is usually experienced with others and it cannot be attained with material items or behaviors. It is ethereal.

"Ironically enough, in the same way that fear brings to pass what one is afraid of, likewise a forced intention makes impossible what one forcibly wishes...

Pleasure is, and must remain, a side-effect or by-product, and is destroyed and spoiled to the degree to which it is made a goal in itself."

Viktor E. Frankl

Think about the most valuable thing you have. Most people's initial, knee-jerk thought is likely something materialistic—perhaps a property, a car, or a collector's item.

While these things do have monetary value, the most valuable thing we have is actually disposable time, not disposable income. What does this mean? It fundamentally leads back to the true pathway to contentment.

MONEY CAN BUY ANYTHING, EXCEPT TIME

The One Thing MasterCard Can't Buy

Many people get pride and pleasure from social recognition, and acceptance from one's peers. Some people are concerned about what others think of them. And one of the ways we achieve these things is through material gains or praise from others for working hard and being successful.

In our society, this is most often measured by how much time is spent working towards these goals. We've all heard of the CEOs and other accomplished people who wake up at 4 A.M. every day in order to be in their position or status level. The simple assumption among almost all of us is: the longer we work, the harder we work, the more money we will make. And money leads to happiness, right?

Wrong! Although wealth and prestige have many benefits, when it comes to contentment, disposable time is what allows us to reinforce our identity and purpose. It gives us the ability to spend quality time with people that we love; to build relationships; and to look after those things that matter to us, such as our health, physical and mental well-being.

There's an African proverb that says: *You have watches, we have time*. When thinking about our journey towards contentment, we can ask ourselves: Do you have a watch, or do you have time?

This is why you should not be searching for constant happiness. This desire leads to a continuous search for pleasure, or for frivolous, superficial things, behaviors, and feelings. You will not find happiness from instant gratification. You will not find happiness from instant thrills. These are all short-term fixes that stimulate dopamine releases, but they don't lead to what you are actually searching for.

★ Instead, you need to strive for contentment. And four specific aspects of your life will determine this contentment. In other words, when you're on your deathbed and you reflect back on your life, these are the four things that are going to decide whether or not you had a content life, or whether or not you are full of regrets.

True Contentment Comes from Authenticity

At the core of the 'search for happiness' is the paradox that one should stop actually searching—externally, at least. Happiness starts with an understanding of oneself, the recognition of your identity and who you truly are, not what you expect others to see or like. The authenticity of who you are (faults included) brings immediate acceptance, peace and the beginning of the road to contentment.

Why is authenticity so fundamental to happiness in life? Many people face a daily conflict within themselves—they struggle to balance who they pretend to be and who they truly are. This is the constant battle between one's true identity and the external image they project to others. It's hard enough to live one life; imagine trying to be someone else as well.

Time and time again, 'successful' people live with a genuine unhappiness that hides behind an image they have carefully crafted and constructed for the outside world—so much so that upholding this façade becomes a daily challenge. With this public image to uphold, there are fewer opportunities to be open and vulnerable.

"Ego says, 'Once everything falls into place, I'll feel peace.' Spirit says, 'Find your peace, and then everything will fall into place.'"

Marianne Williamson

As we've learned about the importance of identity and purpose in one's life, this holds true when it comes to finding contentment. When you are being authentic to your identity and purpose—and not just towards others, but also with yourself—you will start to discover contentment, or that state of satisfaction. That comes from being comfortable with yourself and not putting on a false external image or pretending to be someone you are not. There is no internal conflict in terms of who you are presenting yourself to be externally.

When you start to be your authentic self, it becomes a self-fulfilling prophecy, because through authenticity you become a better version of yourself. You fulfill your potential, because by definition, you are being who you are.

"I prefer to be true to myself, even at the hazard of incurring the ridicule of others, rather than to be false, and to incur my own abhorrence."

Frederick Douglass

Do you know that one person on Facebook who always seems like he or she is having 'the best day ever' every single day? Or how it appears that celebrities or professional athletes have the perfect life, with expensive cars, exotic vacations and successful, lucrative careers?

The world we live in, especially with social media, presents us with an illusion that people should be happy all the time. Sometimes, within a group or even within our own families, we, too, create an illusion of perfection and happiness.

"Perfectionism is a self-destructive and addictive belief system that fuels this primary thought: If I look perfect, and do everything perfectly, I can avoid or minimize the painful feelings of shame, judgment, and blame."

Brené Brown

The problem with this is that people begin to believe that this external image—the one that is constructing the illusion of a happy, fulfilled life—will actually lead to contentment.

You see this by the various examples of people who become consumed with an aspect of their external image, be it physical appearance, physique, social status, or materialistic things. A woman gets plastic surgeries and repeatedly changes her look in her pursuit of happiness through crafting a 'perfect' image, or a man regularly buys expensive designer clothes and posts picture of himself at A-list events in order to portray an image of a lavish lifestyle.

While these external personas make it seem like the individual is content, they will never lead to true happiness because it's all a facade—these perceptions portrayed to people on the outside are never quite the reality.

This creates great internal conflict and confusion for the individual, and the problem with giving the illusion of happiness to others is that sometimes it conceals inner turmoil or depression that could ultimately lead to tragedy, such as suicide or other self-harm.

It's this exact continuous, unfulfilling search and expectation of a perpetual happiness that leads us to just the opposite—dejection and despair. The constant searching will only stop when we accept that there will be storms and things that happen that are simply out of our control. Then, we can focus on the four main elements and arrive at a state of contentment.

Whereas one's identity, purpose, and authenticity will alter and adjust for each individual, there is research on a basic formula that seems to be universal for all human beings. Contemporary positive psychologist Martin Seligman and his associates conducted one of the most interesting surveys on human values, which Seligman later summarized in his 2002 book, *Authentic Happiness*.

What is particularly important about his research is that it studied key values not only across cultures, but also across human history. He identified a large selection of influential writings from different cultures and varying historical periods and presented them to a group of investigators for analysis and summation.

From this review, six fundamental virtues across all cultures and historical time periods emerged:

- **Wisdom:** Curiosity, love of learning, judgment, ingenuity, social intelligence, and perspective

- **Courage:** Valor, perseverance, and integrity

- **Love and humanity:** Kindness, generosity, nurturance, and the capacity to love and be loved

- **Temperance:** Modesty, humility, self-control, prudence, and caution

- **Justice:** Good citizenship, fairness, loyalty, teamwork, and humane leadership

- **Transcendence:** Appreciation of beauty, gratitude, hope, spirituality, forgiveness, humor, and zest

Seligman's central psychological argument is that 'authentic happiness' is built upon the exercise and development of these character virtues—in particular, the identification with some reality or goal beyond oneself. But what happens when the environment changes and suddenly, one's identity and purpose become confusing or unfamiliar because of the shift?

These types of situations happen frequently in cases of retirement, specifically with military veterans or athletes. There are countless examples in sports of men and women who face hardships—financial ruin, emotional trauma, and disintegrating relationships—after an abrupt change in lifestyle and day-to-day motivations and activities.

Six-time Pro Bowl wide receiver Terrell Owens is infamously known for blowing through most of the $80 million he made during his 15-year career in a short period of time after his retirement. A veteran of the NFL for 12 years, defensive lineman

Warren Sapp earned more than $82 million over the course of his career but filed for bankruptcy in 2012.

There are even difficulties for those who don't play professionally. There are an incredible number of high school athletes who are recruited each year into college sports, with a firm belief that they are going to make it to the pros. And when they don't afterwards have a college career, many athletes struggle with the dilemma they are left in.

When the daily practices stop; when game days no longer come; when you are pulled from an environment where other people who share your goals and interests surround you—it's easy to be pushed off the tracks. When your purpose changes, sometimes you need to recalibrate, but that doesn't alter who you are because your identity is established at a young age.

One of the challenges young people growing up today face is the potential for social media to influence and confuse identity and purpose. When someone joins an organization or group, he or she usually latches on to the identity and purpose of that tribe. But when they leave that tribe, those who do not have a strong foundation of identity and purpose established at a young age tend to struggle more often.

Beyond sport, the military is another huge area of concern when it comes to issues spurred by a loss of focus and purpose. In fact, in January 2019, it was reported that the number of confirmed and suspected suicides in the active-duty Marine Corps and the Navy reached a 10-year high in 2018.

The lesson here—no matter military, sport, business, or elsewhere—is that establishing a clear vision of who you are and what your purpose is will lead to greater contentment, especially when you are faced with these types of life shifts.

The Four Keys to Contentment

1. Love Someone and Be Loved

Simply put, you need to both be loved and love others.

I learned a rather surprising lesson in working with some of the most balanced and highest-performing individuals, from CEOs to special operators from around the world, who have found true success in life. The key motivation isn't determination, toughness, or ruthlessness, it is love—a deep affection for family, friends and colleagues.

This love is a desire to care for and see others find peace and contentment. In turn, the reciprocated love serves as motivation and as support when storms appear on the horizon. Truly successful people give love and are loved by others in return.

Again, this is where values underpin relationships—loving those whose values are similar helps you express emotions and build connections with others. And the most important person to love? Yourself.

Many high-achievers who fail to reach this state struggle to love themselves—faults and shortcomings included—but all of these things are crucial to identity.

"Love is that condition in which the happiness of another person is essential to your own."

Robert A. Heinlein

2. Truly Know Thyself

As Bonnie Ware showed us, you will regret the decisions you make if they were made based on someone else's expectations or dreams. Oscar Wilde said it best: "Be yourself; everyone else is already taken."

Knowing who you are and what your identity, or internal image, is based on will help you find peace and contentment. When you understand your role and relationship with the world and can recognize yourself in a larger context, you will be empowered to live the life you have envisioned. Recognize your strengths and opportunities to improve and continue to improve. Don't run from them.

Nobody is perfect. Perfect people aren't authentic. Authentic people aren't perfect. Be yourself, be authentic.

3. Have a Spiritual Model for Life

Those high achievers who have found peace and contentment have a strong model of life and understanding. Whether it is based on stoic philosophy or a religious faith, those who have found contentment have a clearly defined belief system or spiritual model. Beliefs are what we 'know' to be true or what we accept as truth.

While many people inherit a belief system through family and upbringing, religious instruction, popular culture and social interactions, those who have greatest contentment have a robust model for rationalizing life. A belief system is also something I hope this book provides for you—a manual for life and a pathway to contentment in your life and hope.

4. Live a Life to Fulfill Your Life's Purpose

As we have learned from Aristotle, happiness is not an event, but a journey—it's our life, and a life filled with purpose provides fulfillment. You need to have a clear understanding of your identity and fulfill your purpose—you need to have direction in life. People who do this in life avoid a deathbed of regrets when faced with mortality. Purpose provides a clear vision and overarching goals for life.

True contentment comes from living a good or virtuous life, one in the service of others and society. A life where upon reflection, we see that we have not only done the right thing, but the good thing. "He is happy who lives in accordance with complete virtue and is sufficiently equipped with external goods, not for some chance period but throughout a complete life."

"If thou wilt make a man happy, add not unto his riches but take away from his desires."

Epicurus

Ideas for Action

- *Do I confuse pleasure, happiness, and contentment?*

- *Will I have regrets on my deathbed?*

- *Do I love every day to the fullest?*

- *Do I allow myself to be happy?*

- *Do I spend time worrying about what others think of me?*

- *Which matters most, my image or my identity?*

Final Ideas for Action

WHO AM I?

WHAT IS MY PURPOSE?

WHAT IS MY SPIRITUAL MODEL?

WHO DO I LOVE?

WHO LOVES ME?

Afterword

High achievers often grow to confuse preparation with control. They are driven, talented, hard working, and, therefore, have a greater probability of success. But this occasionally leads to a perception of control.

I've seen it repeatedly with everyone from Navy SEALs and CEOs to NFL superstars. The truth is no one is in complete control over anything, except how we respond to events.

Keeping this in mind helps us navigate the challenge that is life. A strong spiritual faith, belief in a high power or system, is central to helping us understand and come to terms with the unexpected or unexplainable.

Truly knowing yourself, understanding who you are, your strengths and limitations, helps you navigate life with the gifts you possess and helps you appreciate that none of us are perfect—regardless of what someone's Instagram profile might try to convince you of.

Your purpose is your fuel. This is the reason you are here and the driving force to impact others around you. Leave a legacy and memory that makes the world for those you love a better place.

Finally, love. No single person can exist or survive alone or without the basic desire to feel necessary or valued, so love and be loved. We all need people, family, and good friends to help us weather the storms of life. When life comes at you fast you will need people whose values you share to help survive the journey.

Be the sheepdog among fellow sheepdogs.

Principles

1. You are not in control of the world. Accept it
2. Never confuse preparation for control
3. You are in control of the one most important thing: your response to life
4. What goes around comes around
5. You are influenced by those you choose to spend the majority of your time with
6. Your survival and success depends on your quality of adaptation
7. Form authentic connections through shared values with people
8. Your contentment depends on first believing the world is a good place
9. Know your concentric circles. Know who is in them
10. Know thy authentic self. Develop authenitc awareness
11. Your why, your purpose is your reason for everything
12. I hate to break it to you. You are not your job
13. Artifacts and behaviors are your values manifested

14. Lead with values, and behaviors take care of themselves
15. Great leaders encourage individuality
16. Great teams have a clear and shared vision
17. Humans are complex adaptive organisms
18. Foundations of psychological wellness influence our belief system
19. Know what you must accept. Know what you can change.
20. The mind and body are one
21. You only get one shot at life. This is neither a drill or a dress rehearsal
22. After the storm, there will be another storm.
23. Always got to the source. Find the why.
24. Sometimes, even a sheepdog needs a sheepdog
25. Refuse to be a victim
26. You will either win or learn. Both are opportunity.
27. Run or hide from your choices and you are destined to repeat them.
28. Resilience is failing fast and furious, then failing differently the next time
29. Authentic people aren't perfect. Perfect people aren't authentic
30. Strive not for happiness. Strive for contentment
31. Authenticity is when your public image and personal identity are aligned
32. Money can buy anything, except time.
33. Know WHO you truly are
34. Understand WHY you are you here
35. Have a Spiritual Model
36. Love and Be Loved

Further Reading

The Art of Living: The Classical Manual on Virtue, Happiness, and Effectiveness; Epictetus and Sharon Lebell

The Complete Works of Epictetus, Epictetus

Letters from a Stoic, Lucius Annaeus Seneca and Robin Campbell

The Essential Writings of Ralph Waldo Emerson, Ralph Waldo Emerson

Meditations, Marcus Aurelius

The Handbook of Epictetus, Epictetus

Philosophy for Life and Other Dangerous Situations: Ancient Philosophy for Modern Problems, Jules Evans

Obstacle Is The Way, Ryan Holiday

Ego Is The Enemy, Ryan Holiday

Daily Stoic, Ryan Holiday

The Story of My Life, Helen Keller

Courage Under Fire: Testing Epictetus's Doctrines in a Laboratory of Human Behavior, James B. Stockdale

Thoughts of a Philosophical Fighter Pilot, James B. Stockdale

Drive: The Story of My Life, Larry Bird

The Analects, Confucius

Discourses and Selected Writings, Epictetus and Robert Dobbin

League of Denial: The NFL, Concussions, and the Battle for Truth; Mark Fainaru-Wada and Steve Fainaru

On Combat: The Psychology and Physiology of Deadly Conflict in War and in Peace, Dave Grossman & Loren W. Christensen

On Killing: The Psychological Cost of Learning to Kill in War and Society, Dave Grossman

Assassination Generation: Video Games, Aggression, and the Psychology of Killing; Lieutenant Colonel Dave Grossman and Kristine Paulsen

Daring Greatly: How the Courage to Be Vulnerable Transforms the Way We Live, Love, Parent, and Lead; Brené Brown

Dare to Lead: Brave Work. Tough Conversations. Whole Hearts, Brené Brown

An Autobiography or The Story of My Experiments with Truth, M. K. Gandhi

Long Walk to Freedom: The Autobiography of Nelson Mandela, Nelson Mandela

A New Earth: Awakening to Your Life's Purpose, Eckhart Tolle

The Four Agreements: A Practical Guide to Personal Freedom, Don Miguel Ruiz

Man's Search for Meaning, Viktor E. Frankl

Game Changer: The Art of Sports Science, Fergus Connolly

59 Lessons: Working with the World's Greatest Coaches, Athletes, & Special Forces; Fergus Connolly

Helping People Win at Work: A Business Philosophy Called "Don't Mark My Paper, Help Me Get an A", Ken Blanchard and Garry Ridge

The Trouble with Testosterone and Other Essays on the Biology of the Human Predicament, Robert M. Sapolsky

Descartes' Error: Emotion, Reason, and the Human Brain; Antonio Damasio

The Power of Habit: Why We Do What We Do in Life and Business, Charles Duhigg

Make Your Bed: Little Things That Can Change Your Life... And Maybe the World, Admiral William H. McRaven

Stress in Health and Disease, Hans Selye

Stress Without Distress, Hans Selye

Stress of Life, Hans Selye

The Polyvagal Theory: Neurophysiological Foundations of Emotions, Attachment, Communication, and Self-regulation; Stephen W. Porges

Tiger Woods, Jeff Benedict and Armen Keteyian

Complete Works of Aristotle, Vol. 1, Aristotle and Jonathan Barnes

Trading Psychology 2.0: From Best Practices to Best Processes, Brett N. Steenbarger

Top Five Regrets of the Dying: A Life Transformed by the Dearly Departing, Bronnie Ware

Flow: The Psychology of Optimal Experience, Mihaly Csikszentmihalyi

TED Talk: "Leadership, Vulnerability and Sheepdogs" by Fergus Connolly

Acknowledgments

Special thank you to my family for their constant love and support. To one of my favorite people, KTM, for helping me create this amazing journey. Jamie Lisanti for all her help and remarkable patience deciphering and clarifying my thoughts, and Stacey Eisenberg for her amazing editing skills.

Special thanks to KMD for teaching me so well. To Ben, Amy, Brian, Lindsay, Derek, Mick, Cam, Bryan, Kent, Nate, Ian, Tom, Matt, Bernard, Yosef, Chris, Joe, Dennis, James, Warren, Stu, Dan, Teena, Craig, Trixy, Meeta, Justin, Mark, Joe, Cody, Pat, Mike, Riley, Ant, Jorge, the SOF guys, and everyone else who have walked this journey with me. Not ordinary sheepdogs: Irish Wolfhounds.

About the Author

Dr. Fergus Connolly is one of the world's leading experts in elite team performance. He has worked with professional sport teams, elite special forces units, and CEO's around the world. Fergus is a keynote speaker and consultant to high–performing organizations.

Learn more at FergusConnolly-dot-com.

Fergus Connolly